"Anthony Randall's new book deserves a wide readership. And we should heed his advice, restore civility in public discourse, and work together to build a better future."

— Lieut. Gen. H.R. McMaster (US Army, Retired), Author of *At War with Ourselves*, *Battlegrounds*, and *Dereliction of Duty*.

"This book is desperately needed right now. Anthony drives home the point that leadership takes moral courage. Standing for what is right is often difficult in our current cultural climate and inevitably comes with personal risk. Anthony takes on that risk himself with this bold exposition of leadership and character. He leads by example utilizing the civility of respectful discourse that he then challenges all of us to embrace as we lead this world forward."

— Josh Phillips, Defensive Assistant Coach NFL Las Vegas Raiders, author of *It's My Time: Learning How to Let God Write Your Story*

"*Practicing Excellence* is a powerful light pointing toward a better future. Anthony Randall brings to this complicated moment in history a fresh, stimulating, and hopeful perspective on how leaders can amplify their positive influence in transforming and elevating society. It is my honor to work with him as an accomplished scholar, military leader, and public intellectual."

— Robert M. Franklin, Laney Professor in Moral Leadership, Emory University, President Emeritus of Morehouse

"As a MLB player, I faced pressure, scrutiny, and the constant demand for peak performance. During my career, Dr. Randall was more than a chaplain and leadership coach; he was a trusted advisor who helped the entire team navigate those challenges with a clear mind and strong character. His deep understanding of leadership and unwavering commitment to excellence had a profound impact on me, both on and off the field. In this book, Dr. Randall delivers the same powerful insights that helped me succeed in the high-stakes world of professional sports. He challenges us to rise above the noise of incivility and mediocrity to lead with courage and embody the values that foster truth and collaboration. His message is not just timely, it's essential for anyone who wants to make a meaningful difference in their community and beyond."

— Ryan Lavarnway, Keynote Speaker, World Series Champion, and Olympian

"In my thirty-year professional career, Anthony is the premier coach and executive leadership trainer. This book is a call-to-action for all Christian, character-based leaders: take ground beyond your workplace into the private square!"

— Michael A. Zara, President of Phillips Tube Group, Inc.

"Once again, Anthony delivers remarkable and revolutionary insights that are based on a true passion for teaching, coaching, and mentoring aspiring and active executives across disciplines in leadership, ethics, excellence, and living a virtuous and purpose driven life."

— Cade Warner, President and CEO of The Westervelt Company

"In a world where the public square is increasingly more intimidating, *Practicing Excellence* provides the playbook for readers to find the moral courage to lead again. Dr. Anthony Randall pulls from his professional experiences of leading and coaching the elite to teach us how to find the elite potential within ourselves through meaningful storytelling, introspective questions for the reader, and the integrations of faith. A bold and necessary read for today's high performers."

— Corie Weathers, LPC, NCC, BCC, Military Clinical Consultant, Author, Lifegiver, LLC

"Anthony has nailed it with this book! The chapter jiu-jitsu speaks to me on the importance of practicing excellence in our art. The approach he takes is very beneficial to martial artist of all styles."

— Professor Jason Keaton, Fourth Degree Brazilian Jiu-Jitsu Black Belt, Owner Blind Fury Jiu-Jitsu

"Anthony not only writes about ethical leadership, embodying one's values, forging excellence, maintaining discipline and empowering leaders; he lives it with passion, enthusiasm, consistency, joy and a good sense of humor."

— Dr. Kim Zovak, Principal, Blue Orchard, ICF Master Certified Coach

"Filled with inspiring heartfelt stories, though-provoking exercises, and character-building advice, *Practicing Excellence* is a must-read for any aspiring leader who strives for human flourishing."

— Kelly Poquiz Burke, Founder & CEO of Career Slay

"Based on our research, one of the top qualities expected of leaders today is role modeling, which encompasses character development, moral education, and ethics. Dr. Anthony Randall not only teaches these principles in his book but also exemplifies them in his own life. From my personal experience with him, he truly embodies and demonstrates what he advocates."

— Dr. Timothy Tirayaki, Founder of Maslow Research Center

"Our society has many needs, but what it needs more than anything is principled and trusted leaders. *Practicing Excellence* provides a road map and is a must read for leaders at all levels and in all professions who want to make a true impact."

— Curt Schaefer, Private Equity Fund Co-Founder and Manager

"Having experienced Dr. Randall's coaching firsthand, I'm struck by his genuine care and integrity. His book *Practicing Excellence* captures the essence of his transformative approach, inspiring leaders to align their passion and purpose. Anthony's wisdom has profoundly impacted my own leadership journey."

— Kinza Azmat, Founder, Chief Rebel

"From the boardroom to the battlefield, I've served with and watched Anthony relentlessly pursue and practice excellence every step of the way. *Practicing Excellence* blends rigorous academic study and practical advice for reigniting and aligning your passion, purpose, and precision."

— Jeff Tiegs, LTC (US Special Forces, Retired)

"Dr. Anthony Randall's book *Practicing Excellence* could not be more timely. Leaders need the courage and skills to face the challenges of leading in today's increasingly divisive society where incivility is common. Dr. Randall challenges the reader to take action with suggested practical advice on steps to be a more effective leader at work and in our personal lives. From the aspiring young leaders to senior executives, from those in leadership development programs to chief executive officers of small and large companies, there is wisdom and insights in *Practicing Excellence* that you can apply today and use to become the most effective leader to affect positive change on your team and in your organization."

— Ken Keen, LTG (US Army, Retired), Associate Dean for Leadership, Emory University
Goizueta Business School

PRACTICING EXCELLENCE

Restoring Civility, Faith & Trusted

Leadership in the Public Square

PRACTICING EXCELLENCE

Restoring Civility, Faith & Trusted

Leadership in the Public Square

Dr. Anthony Randall

FP
HOUSE

This title has been catalogued with the Library of Congress

First Edition – October 2024
Paperback ISBN: 979-8-3303-9496-8
Hardcover ISBN: 979-8-3303-7041-2

PRINTED IN THE UNITED STATES OF AMERICA

ephouse.co

To Jeanine, Aria, William, and John,
for your unconditional love, grace, and sacrifice in pursuing
God's call on our lives together
as servant leaders and warrior shepherds.
Relentlessly hunt down the wolves and protect the flocks!

To my mentors, friends, and brothers and sisters in arms,
thank you for your courage, wisdom, love, and friendship.

To the United States Army
for providing me a life well lived serving God, country,
and the next generation of trusted professionals.

To what lies ahead,
may it be a pursuit of excellence and human flourishing,
loving God, loving people, and finding joy
in the sanctifying process.

Contents

⋯ List of Abbreviations

AEWE – Army Expeditionary Warrior Experiment
BCT – Brigade Combat Team
CAPE – Center for the Army Professional Ethic
CDIC – Character Development Instructor Course
ESCI – Emotional Social Competency Inventory
HOPE – Human Optimization Performance Enhancement
MBTI – Myers-Briggs Type Indicator
MCCC – Maneuver Captain's Career Course
MCOE – Maneuver Center of Excellence
NCO – Non-Commissioned Officer
PME – Professional Military Education
TML – Transformational Moral Leadership

··· Prologue

"You're an 'Anthony' not a 'Tony.'" My second-generation Italian mother emphatically began shaping my character at a young age. She wanted me to ensure I knew who I was called to become. She taught me character, values, and virtue, a love for people, and how to laugh.

Ironically, the only place I was ever called "Tony" was during my four years at the United States Military Academy, West Point, training to become a leader of character. I took my family to my twentieth class reunion and when my children heard my friends calling me Tony, my ten-year-old son exclaimed, "Dad, I don't think these people know who you are." Through passionate, purposeful, and precise practice, I hope I have become a transformational leader of character who continues to pursue excellence, practices transformation, and promotes human flourishing.

Who am I? How do I think? How do I lead? You will be asked these "3 Qs of Who" throughout this book. You will be challenged to assess how your practice makes permanent, not perfect. You will be encouraged to aspire to living a life of excellent practice.

Me? I'm a great grandson of an immigrant shoemaker from Naples, Italy, and an eighth generation grandson of a Massachusetts militiaman who fought at Lexington-Concord, firing some of the first shots against the British and initiating the American Revolution. My belief in the ideas represented in the Constitution of the United States of democracy, freedom, virtue, faith, liberty, and justice led to a twenty plus year military career, where I was privileged to serve with some of the most elite units in the world as a shooter and shepherd—a Ranger and a chaplain.

My Christian belief in human flourishing influences my conviction, like Dr. Martin Luther King Jr., that the Apostle Paul is correct. We are to live a life of sacrifice, being transformed by the renewing of our minds and giving us passionate courage, purposeful clarity, and a precise cause to challenge the conformity of this world as transformed non-conformists. Practicing excellence is a lifelong endeavor. It isn't easy and not everyone does it, because it's the hard daily routine.

Thirty years of martial arts trained me to embrace the martial way, practicing a "white belt mentality" of continual growth through intentional practice and rigorous training. At fifty years old, motion is lotion, especially after seven surgeries. I travel with my gi, always ready to roll. Thirty years of failing, succeeding, transforming, and changing as a leader of character has taught me who I am, how I think, and how I lead epistemologically. Today, my passion and purpose are to challenge leaders to consider how to do that with precision and practicing excellence.

I've conversed in some of the most progressively liberal "inclusive" classrooms of higher education, that were quite "exclusive," until my fellow classmates took time to find out who I really was as a leader of character. I've smoked cigars around firepits with some of the most staunchly conservative civic leaders, who inclusively welcomed me in because of my background, yet at times excluded me when I challenged them to expand their worldviews. I've lived, trained, laughed, and shed tears with some of the most elite warriors in the world, who sacrificed their lives protecting freedom and democracy from global terrorism. I have celebrated the thrill of victory and agony of defeat with players, coaches, and staff of professional and college sports teams. I've led and coached everywhere from the battlefield to the boardroom. Through these lenses, I have watched our esteemed public squares, marketplaces, communities, and houses of worship deteriorate into arenas of incisive incivility, insecure identities, indignant arrogance, myopic intellect, and unaccountable individualism.

I began observing these trends with greater detail nearly ten years ago, as I pursued graduate and post-graduate degrees in ethics, philosophy, character development, and transformational leadership, while teaching ethics and leadership for the United States Army. And I continue to encounter it today as my company, Vanguard XXI, teaches and trains leadership development and professional coaching.

Our nation's civic public square, founded upon the virtues of classic liberalism, is being destroyed by the vices of religious totalitarianism and progressive secularism. Educated derelicts, bully pulpits, talking heads, and a society overloaded with mass information lacks the critical thinking to process and apply pragmatic application and has blunted moral courage to faithfully live lives as transformational leaders. They have baffled the clear mind in favor of confuted worldviews and exchanged truths for lies. They have burdened the soul, removing a need for spirituality and making politics their god. Our nation, young and old, is being numbed into accepting mediocrity, fearful of being canceled or criticized for pursuing a life of excellence. We have a leadership crisis of character necessitating a call to action. We must teach and train moral agents of character to lead as trusted professionals. We must reclaim the civility of the public square with virtuous intent, critical thinking, and courageous action.

My passion is to relentlessly transform the public square back to a place of civility. A public square where people pursue who they are, practicing a life of virtue and encouraging others to do the same. A public square where people's minds are transformed through practicing excellence in *how* to think, not conformed in *what* to think, and remain open to how others think differently. A public square where leaders lead morally and ethically, with emotional intelligence, pursuing human flourishing, and seeing people as the end state and not a means to their own narcissistic ends.

We must passionately, purposefully, and precisely pursue what it means to teach, train, and live lives practicing excellence, restoring civility, faith, and trusted leadership in the public square. My hope is that this book inspires you to join me in doing this important work.

— Anthony Randall

··· PART I: Ethos

Courageous Character

··· Chapter One: White Belt Mentality

It's July 4th, 1986. I was twelve years old and the youngest paper boy in Denver, Colorado, delivering the *Rocky Mountain News*. I was folding papers on my workbench, sliding them into plastic sleeves and loading them into my canvas newspaper carriers wrapped around the handles of my Huffy BMX Pro Thunder bike. I was pumped because I love the Fourth of July. My mornings started out this way every day, except in the Colorado winters when I had to carry them over my shoulders and walk through the snow … uphill … both ways. (IYKYK) We lived in a subdivision where every garage and six-foot wooden fence was built the same way. With a rhythmic peddling of my bike, I reached for a paper and tossed it over the fence, listening for the crisp whack of it hitting the three-by-three foot concrete pad in front of the garage door. The apartments were more difficult, especially the guy on the second floor who wanted it on his balcony.

I was learning as a young entrepreneur to "sell deep," as I discovered my paper route provided additional business opportunities when I built trust and respect with my clients. I practiced civility with customers, built faithful relationships, and earned trust. I didn't expect to face adversity.

That day, what started as a beautiful Colorado morning and promised a great day ahead, celebrating liberty and freedom, has a surprise for me. I was in a good rhythm, kicking some nineties jams on my knock off Sony Walkman, tossing and delivering papers left and right. Out of the corner of my eye I noticed a Volkswagen Bug, full of teenagers, pulling up and trailing me. They threatened me and demanded a newspaper. I conceded, steered my bike off the sidewalk, across the grass and onto the street. Out of the passenger window flashed a red cylinder. I instinctively grabbed a newspaper and held it up to my face as I was doused from head to toe in fire extinguisher retardant. It was not the explosive Fourth of July I had in mind.

I cried all the way home, full of shock and fear, and told my parents what happened. While concerned about my safety, they asked if I had finished my route. I had not, but needed to. My character was threatened as adversity hit me literally right in the face, and my disciplined obedience to continue was challenged. I finished my route that day, and every day after for the next two and a half years, continuing to grow my newspaper business. I learned, as a twelve-year-old CEO, lessons that still apply to executive leaders today.

The public square is a dangerous place. Character counts, so leaders must know who they are, how they think, and how they lead. Leaders must learn to overcome adversity. Leaders should know how to train their trust and trust their training. Leaders of character pursue lives of disciplined obedience, willing to show up, play up, and finish in a volatile, uncertain, chaotic, and ambiguous world. Accountability drives ownership and ownership drives accountability. What virtues guide you in an uncivil public square? What adversity are you prepared to face and overcome with faithfulness? How do you maintain disciplined obedience to practice excellence with passion, purpose, and precision in a world of mediocrity as a trusted leader?

Our nation's civic public square, founded upon the virtues of classic liberalism, is under attack and has become uncivil. We have a leadership crisis of character, and it necessitates a call to action. We must teach and train moral agents of character to lead as trusted professionals. We must restore the civility of the public square with virtuous intent, moral and ethical thinking, and courageous leadership. As Plato's Meno challenged Socrates, thousands of years ago, we are challenged by the same questions today: How do you teach and train leaders of character? How do you teach critical thinking and decision making? How do you coach and lead character and culture by pursuing excellence? How can human flourishing and civility reclaim the public square?

I can clearly see the beginning of my journey, sitting at my parents' kitchen table. Our eighties carpet, a blend of browns and oranges, complimented the brick façade and wood paneling of our kitchen nook walls. The Army recruiter sat across from me in one of our seventies table chairs, with black leather seat and a wooden high back. He slid a marketing trifold across the table for me to peruse.

"US Army. Be All You Can Be."

It was the summer of 1991, just after Operation Desert Storm, and the US Army was recruiting a professional volunteer force based upon attracting and appealing to young men and women who desired to stretch themselves, grow, prove what they were made of, and serve a higher cause than their own. I opened the marketing trifold. Its three frames displayed the teaching and training I could receive, and if successful, what I could become. "Airborne," followed by a paratrooper descending under full parachute canopy. "Ranger," followed by a Ranger submerged chest deep patrolling through a swamp with his weapon. "Special Forces," followed by a Green Beret camouflaged from head to toe and doing something cool. (Green Berets always get to do the cool stuff.) I looked at the recruiter.

"I want to do all three," I finally said. "How do I do that?"

He smiled, slowed me down, and began to explain.

"Well, this is how it works…" and began sharing the fine print that I could not sign up to do all three right away, or maybe even at all, depending on what I enlisted for.

He was right, I was impatient. I asked him to leave.

Later that year, I applied to attend the United States Naval Academy, Annapolis, and the United Stated Military Academy, West Point. The Navy said, "No." But the Army said, "Well, since two other better qualified candidates turned down their appointments (I was a third alternate to West Point), we will offer you an appointment on the last possible day." I graciously took the appointment. (Go Army! Beat Navy! It was a good choice. Our class won the Army Navy Football Game, four years in a row. I started as the twelfth man every year, up in the stands cheering on the Brave Old Army Team. I still have season tickets.)

Over the course of my twenty plus year career, I had the fortunate opportunity to test the rigors of the Army's various teaching and training models. I graduated (barely) from West Point. I failed Advanced English, earned a D in Chemistry, and Cs and C-s peppered my transcript. I barely maintained a 2.0 GPA after my first two years, but over the next two years, through teaching and training, I graduated on the Dean's List. I graduated from the Army's Command and General Staff College and was selected for Advanced Civil Schooling to earn an additional graduate degree and become an Army Ethics Instructor. I graduated from multiple special operations courses, like S.E.R.E. (Survival, Evasion, Resistance, and Escape), that further tested my character, intellect, emotional and physical stamina under duress.

Practice. Practice. Practice.

Following graduation from West Point, I headed to Ft. Benning (now renamed Ft. Moore), Georgia, for additional character development, called the US Army Ranger School, affectionately known as "not for the weak or fainthearted." I was unaware then, that twenty years later I would be back at Ft. Moore, and at the forefront of shaping the next generation in leadership and character development, to work at the Ranger School as the senior chaplain. I accomplished two of those trifold dreams, becoming Airborne—a Master Parachutist, even—and a US Army Ranger. I graduated from the 62-Day US Army Ranger School, in one hundred and twenty days, after recycling two phases. More practice. And I was fortunate and blessed to serve in Engineer, Infantry, Cavalry, Airborne, Ranger, Special Forces, and special operations units throughout my career, including multiple combat tours to Afghanistan and Iraq.

Painful and powerful practice.

Fifteen of those twenty plus amazing years were spent as a chaplain. As an Army ethics curriculum developer and instructor, I had the opportunity to consolidate twenty years of teaching, training, and practicing permanence into a leadership character development and coaching process to transform leaders and forge excellence.

The Maneuver Center of Excellence (MCOE) at Ft. Moore is home to the infantry and armor schools, the 75th Ranger Regiment, and specialty schools such as Ranger, airborne, sniper, and Pathfinder. MCOE trains 69,000 officers, non-commissioned officers (NCOs), and soldiers a year. Since 1918, Ft. Moore has been known as the Army's epicenter to teach and train combat leaders. The warrior ethos and warrior soul are forged there. It is the Army's "Tip of the Spear" for training the warrior ethos. It was the breeding ground of practice through thousands of sets and reps for validating the transformational moral leadership and coaching model you will experience in this book. Today, it is humbling to know the curriculum developed and implemented in 2016 at MCOE is now the standardized curriculum for character and leadership development teaching and training thousands of US and Allied Army Officers every year. (Hang in there. This just isn't a little green Army guy story.)

We've made some IOS updates and today's Vanguard Way is like an iPhone 15 in comparison to the first one Steve Jobs held in his hand in 2007, or what I taught in 2016. The principles of practicing excellence, and aligning passion, purpose, and precision in how we teach, train, and flourish as human beings transcend industries and professions. Through building trusted relationships, maintaining a growth mindset, and a relentless practice of sets and reps in leadership opportunities, today it is humbling to provide leadership development and coaching in a myriad of marketplaces.

We actively lead, coach, teach, and train leaders in the corporate marketplace from Fortune 100 to 1000 companies, private capital equity firms, manufacturing, sales, small and medium size businesses, and different government branches from hospitals to special operations units to the FBI. This includes eight amazing years in Major League Baseball working with coaches, players, and front office personnel, and two years in NCAA Division I men's basketball, to include national championship and runner up teams. Life is good; never a dull moment.

Now, all those stories will not fit into a nineties US Army marketing trifold. However, the process of practicing excellence *does* fit in this book.

Practicing Excellence. Promoting Human Flourishing.

Together, we will explore the art and science of transformational leadership development and practicing the art of coaching people and organizations to pursue excellence. You will be introduced to a leadership development, a coaching model that is shaping high performance organizations of over 15,000 professionals across global marketplaces and industries. Practicing a life of excellence, pursuing virtue, and promoting human flourishing is a lofty, and accomplishable goal … and it requires practice. Practicing excellence builds upon the philosophy that practice makes permanent, not perfect. Therefore, leaders must pursue practice that is passionate, purposeful, and precise.

Throughout history, people pursued human flourishing through epistemological studies, i.e., philosophically pursuing knowledge with critical thinking through the lenses of theology, ethics, mathematics, science, logic/reason, history, and experience. Yes, along with slang phrases and everyday vernacular, some chapters have big words and big ideas, such as epistemology. We still study one of the most important professions of human flourishing critical to the moral, ethical, and just conduct of any tribe or nation state: the warrior profession and professional soldier's ethic. The US military's aggressive pursuit to optimize service members' performance must include the assessment, teaching, training, caring, and forging of the professional warrior soul. It begins with character development and identity from self to service, and even something bigger than you.

The pursuit of high-performance talent management spans professions and industries. You likely experienced from your own perspective how the post-COVID global marketplace endured the "great resignation" and "great remorse." We saw the true character, reasoning, leadership, and fragility or anti-fragility of people and organizations exposed for better or worse. Now, leaders like you, who pursue excellence, are postured for the "great recruitment." This is a metaphysical state of being found in the human soul and seeking a life of practicing excellence aligned with their passion, purpose, and precision of who they are, how they think, and what type of leaders they desire to become. Great talent wants back in the game.

So, how do you attract, assess, develop, promote, and retain it?

The Vanguard XXI leadership development and coaching model is forged out of twenty-seven years of rigorous academic and pragmatic application of assessing, developing, practicing, and retaining high performance talent based upon developing leaders of character. Developing leaders of character, building high performance cultures, and creating the chemistry and climate for belonging, growth, and achieving excellence is necessary in any public square, marketplace, community, organization, team, or family. The lessons learned and methodologies applied here translate and correlate to any professional marketplace.

Transformational moral leadership presents a coaching, teaching, and training methodology consisting of virtue ethics, moral reasoning, ethical decision making, and emotionally intelligent leadership. Such an approach aims to achieve the end state of mitigating immoral, unethical behavior, and promoting trusted leaders of character who shape culture and influence climates of high performing organizations as trusted professionals.

My vision is that transformational moral leadership engages, elevates, expands, refines, and forges people of excellence through moral courage, moral reasoning, and moral empathy. My mission is to transform leaders, forge excellence, and empower leaders to win. I wrote that vision statement in 2015 for a graduate thesis at Emory University. It includes the three pillars of transformational moral leadership. I recognized my coaching process embedded within this work during my doctoral work a few years later at Fuller Seminary. I reflected upon the question, "How do I coach?" and there it was sitting right in front of me, embedded within my thesis statement, waiting for me to discover it. When the student is ready, the teacher appears. Now, this book isn't a coaching session. However, these five steps will guide you through this book, further empowering you as a leader of character, a thought leader, and a leader of influence. By the end of this chapter, my goal is that you are engaged and elevated to a position to learn and grow. The remainder of the book will then expand, refine, and forge your journey.

Engage enables coaches and clients to be where their feet are at in a client focused and psychologically safe environment, ready to grow. Where are your feet at as you prepare to read this book? There are some questions at the end of this chapter that you may find helpful in answering that question.

Elevate. This creates a space for leaders to focus on the most important areas of growth at hand, identify the value behind these areas of growth, set outcomes, and have clarity. What kind of space are you creating to identify what you want out of reading, or listening, to this book? What's important to you about pursuing and practicing a life of excellence? You will discover a few questions at the end of chapter to guide you.

Expand with each lesson. Each chapter may stand on its own, however, when read comprehensively, this book will challenge you to reflect on your character, experiences, and the virtues and values that ground you. It will challenge you to critically think through a moral and ethical lens on how you and other leaders have made decisions, and where you may seek growth and improvement. Ask yourself what emotional and mental shifts are taking place, and why. What are the challenges or affirmations behind your thoughts and emotions? Remain open-minded. Be curious. It will enlighten you and provide a new perspective on leading yourself, high character people, and high functioning cultures.

Refine. Take notes. Use the margins. What changes will you make to practice excellence differently? How will you cognitively and critically develop your own methodology of practicing excellence? How will you refine your decision-making processes? What will you identify as strengths in your current practice? Where are your gaps? How do you grow? What trusted leaders of character are in your life? Who has permission to challenge and support you? What other resources do you require?

Forge. At the end of the book, you will once again be challenged to reflect on how you will finish well, live a life well lived, and practice excellence. Put your plan into action. We did. You will find research and our approach to teaching and training character and transformational leadership in the epilogue.

Finally, connect. We want to celebrate beside you. Connect and let's finish well together! Our mission is to empower leaders and organizations to assess, develop, practice, and retain high performance leaders of character and build high performance cultures by facilitating climates of personal, professional, and industry growth through leadership development and coaching. Leadership development, in conjunction with leadership coaching, creates an integrated relationship between employee engagement and performance management. Or, as my friend and business associate Tim Tiryaki says, "Leadership development without coaching is just entertainment." It requires a collaborative relationship.

This book is a guide for you, the trusted professional, a trusted agent of character, to navigate the volatile, uncertain, complex, and ambiguous

(VUCA) environments. COVID was a volatile shock to our fragile social, political, and economic systems. It was merely a microwave, creating uncertainty and lack of trust between fellow citizens and supposed trusted leaders of character and institutions. It accelerated social, political, and economic complexity in the public square, and likely your respective marketplace today. Maybe you're tackling some of these questions as a result.

So, how do leaders clarify the ambiguity of today's challenging marketplace conditions with adaptive and transformational leadership? Your journey through this book will help you answer questions like these.

How do leaders pursue excellence through talent management in a remote or hybrid work environment? How will you implement it? We will share our approach to character development, coaching, and empowering people's innate desire to flourish in any environment.

How do leaders improve employee engagement? Through coaching leadership development and creating a common language. One of the greatest employee engagement feedback items a Fortune 100 client ever received reported their leaders were doing more coaching and less directing, thereby empowering subordinate leaders and teams in a remote, hybrid environment. We will share with you the process we shared with them.

How do leaders influence alignment of individual and corporate values, mission, and vision with a growing transitory workforce? It begins with what we call the "3 Qs of Who." They apply to individuals and organizations.

The tenets of practicing excellence will improve your talent management process from assessment and selection, to training and development, to promotion and retention. With practice, it will engage, elevate, expand, refine, and forge your leadership and coaching philosophy and practical effectiveness as a trusted leader of character. *Practice Excellence. Practice Makes Permanent. Be All You Can Be.*

White Belt Mentality

What kind of belt are *you* wearing? According to tradition, Sensei Jigaro Kano, the father of modern-day Judo, when asked by his students on his death bed what were his last requests, he had only one.

"Bury me in my white belt."

Yeah. *What's behind that?*

One of the greatest modern day martial artists, a master of practicing permanence and excellence of the martial way, a black belt of the highest degree, asked to be buried in his white belt. In martial arts, that's not a fashion statement. It's not what holds up your pants. It is the beginner's belt and represents a student's open mind as an empty cup, ready to be filled and prepared to learn. In martial arts we call it the "white belt mentality." In sportsy psychology and human performance it is referred to as a growth mentality or being a lifelong learner.

I'm leaning in on the assumption you picked up this book because you are a lifelong learner pursuing a growth mentality. Sensei Kano was the same way. He followed up his white belt request by explaining to his students his reasoning. Sensei Kano believed that since he came into this world as a learner, he also wanted to leave this world as a learner. Even though he was rightfully a black belt in character, skill, and experience, he held onto a white belt mentality as a practitioner of permanence and excellence until his last breath.

In the coaching industry, we speak about establishing a proper coaching foundation. It begins with the ethical practice of creating a coaching mindset creating a safe psychological environment to be open, curious, adaptable, and client focused. We co-create a relationship through agreements and trust. We communicate effectively through active listening and evoking awareness. And finally, we are committed to cultivating the client's learning and growth. What if the public square could operate that way again?

As we begin this journey together, even though you may be on a flight to Dallas and I may be leading a course in Atlanta, take a moment for yourself. A tactical pause in an overly busy world to consider your mindset and posture as you begin to dive into practicing excellence with passion, purpose, and precision. This is an opportunity for the two of us to connect with one another, as if we are sitting together in 14A and 14B. Sure, I'll take the middle seat if you prefer the aisle or window.

Remember: engage, elevate, expand, refine, and forge.

Here we go.

What belt am I wearing, and why?

_____

_____

What would I like to better understand about myself?

_____

_____

_____

Where would I like to grow in my leadership and coaching philosophy and skill?

_____

_____

How will growing in my leadership and coaching benefit people?

_____

_____

What mental/emotional "blocks" do I need to remove to embrace a growth mindset while reading this book?

_____

_____

_____

Who may I seek to better know, trust, rely, and commit to as a fellow leader and coach as I apply what I learn in this book?

_____

_____

_____

What kind of mental shift has just occurred for you? What emotional adjustment did you experience? How have you gained more clarity? Just a couple more questions before we start our journey—three to be exact. And yes, I'm going to ask you a lot of questions in this book so keep that pen and paper handy. I'm following you on this journey, but this book was written for you.

Be attuned in the moment (A.I.M.) Where is your focus today?

_____

_____

_____

What's important to you *right now*? (W.I.N.)

_____

_____

_____

Finally, end state (END). What is your desired outcome from reading this book?

_____

_____

_____

Great job. Are you ready to take the next step?

··· Chapter Two: Poker Bros &
Consummate Pros

I've taught, trained, and served over twenty-seven years in the military, corporate America, law enforcement, professional and college sports, academia, the martial arts, and more. Across time and space, I have found one thing to be true: leaders of character drawn to certain professions adhere to, define, and defend the ethos of that profession. They hold themselves accountable and allow others to hold them accountable to the defined professional ethos. Leaders of character take ownership of an ethos as moral agents of their profession. Accountability drives ownership and ownership drives accountability. Consummate professionals identify, reflect, and build upon defining experiences that shaped them as trusted professionals. When speaking to audiences, I often ask them to reflect on their own defining moments of becoming a professional.

One friend experienced this during his rookie year playing Major League Baseball when he hit his first home run at Wrigley Field. Another friend worked tirelessly at earning his PhD, was hired as a full-time university professor, and earned tenure. Completing seminary, passing ordination boards, and getting hired as a senior pastor of a church can take several years of practice and preparation. Receiving a commission as an officer in the military is a special day and swearing to an oath to defend an ideal and way of life greater than oneself. For my fellow veterans and me, being tested under fire and surviving combat was a defining moment.

I have a garage gym—or a "box," as CrossFitters call it—that includes a dojo with mats, heavy bag, etc. In front of the squat rack hangs the picture of my Army Ranger Class 5-97 and a photo of my Ranger squad, four of whom I stay in close contact with. Two of them I work beside in my company. Trust me, we had some defining moments together ... good, bad, and ugly ... that provide us great memories and good humor when we see each other. When I stare at that photo, my fellow Rangers stare back at me and all excuses fade away. And I hear myself think, *Get under the bar. Add load. Proper form. Do the work. Never skip a leg day.* Becoming Rangers further defined our unique ethos as soldiers and the profession of arms. It gave us a greater sense of accountability and ownership as we practiced and progressed into other professions. We all have defining moments that shape who we are as professionals.

When did you know *you* were a professional? What event or events defined it? Who validated you? Who relied upon you because of your expertise? What certification did you receive? What success did you experience? What did it feel like to cash that first paycheck?

However, moral agents within a profession still have a choice. We can undergo all the required professional training, and yet at times, as morally autonomous agents, we can intentionally or unintentionally violate the very ethos we are trusted to uphold. We can violate the trust of a profession and fellow professionals. How do professions hold those who violate the professional ethos accountable? How do those professionals have an opportunity to be reinstated? We will dive deeper into the psychology behind this and some real-world examples later in the book.

Trust is a non-negotiable attribute in any healthy relationship. Raise your hand if you've broken someone's trust within an ethos. Raise your hand if someone has broken yours. If we were in a room together, you would see everyone raising both hands. Breaking the trust of an individual or an organization is one of the greatest ways we can fail ourselves and others. How others hold us accountable to take ownership and how we respond are paramount in successfully reestablishing ourselves as trusted professionals within a trusted profession.

Maybe, you're like me. Maybe failure, not success, are the most defining moments in your professional journey. How did you learn what it meant to be a professional by failing … miserably? Let's consider that versus all the success stories we could talk about. Let's talk about failing as a professional, and the transformational change that can occur through failure when we and others take accountability and ownership.

Poker Bros

I like to play cards. No. Not Spades, Uno, Rook, Uecker, or Go Fish. I grew up *playing cards.* It all began in my friend's basement sophomore year of high school. Penny Poker. We played together for several years through high school and when we were all home for the holidays during college; John Boy, Boo, Chris, Fro, Jose, JB, Alex, and Action Ants (that's me). Today, you wouldn't recognize us by those names, and we will keep it that way to protect the innocent. Through success and failure, we figured out how to be professionals in our own right and find successful careers adhering to professional codes of ethics. Today we are a career government civil servant, corporate executive, professional engineer, university professor, corporate sales executive, and a senior law enforcement officer. Poker bros to trusted pros.

I was a pretty good card player. More good than pretty (looks can be deceiving). My first Army assignment was as a student at the Engineer Officer Basic Course at Ft. Leonardwood, Missouri. Unless you are an avid outdoorsman, there was not a lot to keep young second lieutenants busy on the weekends. So, we played cards. It started out just four of us with a nickel, dime, quarter, and sometimes a ten or twenty dollar buy in. These were beer and pizza easy-going Friday nights. Then, the word spread, and more people wanted to play. The problem was, they were not as good as Simpy, Suc, Jaime, and me. By the end of every night, we were typically up—substantially. All above board and fair, no cheating … just a lot of bad poker players. (At least they got free beer and pizza!)

One day, the four of us thought, *what if we had a competition to see who could win the most money?* Not on a Friday night, but rather a full twenty-four hour span—with no sleep from Saturday morning to Sunday morning—onboard a river boat casino in St. Louis, drinking all the complimentary "Diet Pepsi" that casinos provide winners. You get the drift. I wasn't exactly making it to church on time back then. Did any of our peers hold us accountable or stop us? Did they ever challenge our thinking? Of course not. Instead, they wanted to know how much we won each weekend, if there was a game that Friday night, and if they could come with us to St. Louis. I typically answered those questions rather quickly. "Yes!" "Yes, of course, bring a friend," and "Um, yeah, that's a hard 'no.'"

Collectively, our little band of bros won a strong five figures in four months. I had to file state and federal taxes on my "earnings." (I didn't even know you could get taxed on your gambling earnings until then.) I bought my wife's engagement ring with a stack of Ben Franklins. True story. I could have filmed a music video flipping a deck of Benjamins at the jeweler, Rabbi Jay. Think Beastie Boys meets Army lieutenant with a high and tight haircut and a rabbi in a jewelry shop. Straight to the top of the charts.

Six months later, I graduated from the Army's Ranger School and was assigned as a young engineer officer to an airborne infantry battalion in the 82nd Airborne Division. I was a fish out of water and trying to fit in. In the military, you are typically the main effort or the support effort. Supporters are always trying to fit in and prove their value and worth to the team. Most high-performance organizations have similar social circles.

The outside sales reps get to do all the high-end events with clients and conferences, while they are supported by the inside sales team or customer fulfillment call center, hunkered down in cubicles. The c-suite and Executive Leadership Teams (ELT) make all the critical decisions, and the HR professional fights for an equal seat and voice at the table, much like the hard-working plant manager battling daily to be heard and valued by corporate leaders. I was in the unit for only a few weeks when we deployed for an operational planning exercise as staff to Ft. Polk, Louisiana. Like Ft. Leonardwood, there is nothing to do there, especially when you are on temporary duty orders.

One evening, I broke a twenty-dollar bill on a BBQ sandwich and soda, put more than fifteen dollars of change in my pocket, and proceeded back to the barracks where my fellow lieutenant and captain staff officers were staying. This was the crowd I wanted to be a part of. I wanted to earn their trust and be on the team. I wanted a seat at the table, to earn the right to be heard and be one of the guys. As I walked down the hallway, I heard a ruckus coming from one of the rooms. I poked my head in to see beer, pizza, and several guys playing nickel, dime, quarter poker. They called out to me as the "new guy." I'll leave the other colorful military nicknames I was called out of the story. They asked me if I played cards and I said, "a little bit."

Three hours later, I walked away with over eight hundred dollars in my pocket: checks, cash, and several IOUs. We didn't have CashApp or Venmo back then. What did I *not* walk out of there with? Friends. More importantly, trust. In my earnest to prove I could be part of the team and hold my own, I cleaned those guys out when I didn't *have* to. I could have folded a few hands. I could have gone easy. But I didn't. They may have paid me in cash and checks, but I paid in losing their trust. You may be thinking I didn't do anything wrong, right? Wrong. I broke unwritten rules of the warrior code. I took advantage of guys who I was supposed to fight beside and be their friend. Many times, organizationally unaware leaders can break or violate written or unwritten rules. Maybe you're reading this reflecting on how you've developed, compromised, adapted, and solidified your moral compass as a professional. Maybe you're asking yourself, "What is my moral compass?" as you reflect on where you are in life as a leader. Perhaps you're even asking yourself, "What does it mean to be a professional?"

Recently, in a short twenty-four hour period, three news stories came across my social media feed that highlighted the need for these questions as morally autonomous individuals who ascribe to be a part of a professional ethos. NBA basketball player, Jontay Carter, banned for life for betting on his own sport. Amazon's ethically questionable secret operation to gather intelligence on rivals causing a moral dilemma for those hired to do so. And Google fired twenty-eight employees for protesting company deals with Israel. *What is going on here?*

The tension we experience as leaders who pursue human flourishing, through our moral autonomy, arises when we agree to support a heteronomous ethos. It's like signing a contract with a company or a professional sports team. We wear their logo on our uniform, we attach our names to company email addresses, we have an email signature block, and we get paid for our services. When we transition from amateurs living our own way of life to professionals exercising who we are, how we think, and how we lead, we acknowledge our moral beliefs align to a larger extent with a greater organizational ethic. We create what should be a healthy tension between being individually accountable to our own moral code, and by our own volition, align ourselves with a greater organizational ethic that will hold us accountable to take ownership of. We will experience internal and external alignment and occasional conflict with people who agree or disagree with our moral codes, however, we all agree collectively to the greater ethic.

Regardless of where you stand on these three articles, the tension for transformational leaders remains. Who you are, how you think, and how you lead as a professional leader of character impacts who you are, how your profession is trusted, and who directly or indirectly benefits from you and your organization. When I ask this question in our leadership coaching courses, participants come up with excellent responses that align with other courses who are asked the same question. They highlight character attributes and values such as integrity, trust, courage, agility, initiative, and teamwork. They mention because someone told them they were a professional or a subject matter expert due to their certifications, qualifications, and performance. Many times, the last marker mentioned is being paid for services. That always warms my heart. Being a professional means begins with you becoming a trusted leader of character.

This was where I went astray that night playing poker, and I knew it. I knew better; to choose the "harder right" over the "easier wrong." But my pride and ego got the best of me. Attempting to adhere to the new social construct of my peers, I experienced a moment of moral bravado rather than moral courage on my part. This included poor moral reasoning and a lack of understanding the influence of emotionally intelligent leadership. Violations of a personal moral code and a professional ethic occurred. This moment was key to my forging process as an elite professional warrior. Learning the written and unwritten rules of any organization is key.

I was not the only one who made a mistake that night. The next morning, our battalion commander addressed the young officers collectively, simply stating that we should be ashamed of ourselves as a group of professionals. Then he singled them out for trying to take advantage of the "new guy," telling them they received exactly what they deserved by losing their money. I was relieved; he'd taken my side! Or so I initially thought. It turned out, I was wrong. He eventually singled me out as a morally autonomous agent, saying, "Lt. Randall, that's *not* what we do."

Our battalion commander became a mentor for many of us throughout our careers. He retired as a four-star general after serving as the Vice Chief of Staff of the US Army. One of Gen. (Ret.) Dan Allyn's best quotes was, "You can't surge character." No sir, you cannot. Thank you for that life lesson so long ago. Fast forward twenty years from that night and my commander's son is now commissioned as a second lieutenant in the US Army. He attended my ethics course as a young infantry officer, where I regularly share this story with young leaders. When he told his dad I shared this story, his dad told him to tell me to keep telling it. It is a self-regulating professional ethos.

Any profession exists and endures because of professionals who exercise moral courage, reasoning, and empathy to create transformational legacies by shaping other leaders and self-regulating the warrior ethos. Today, many of those young officers are senior Army leaders, general officers, and executive leaders in the marketplace. We've not played poker together since that night; however, we have found common ground on leadership development, coaching, and holding one another accountable as professionals. Defining moments occur throughout a professional's career, and further clarifies their character, competence, and commitment. Such moments challenge a professional's obedience to their own moral code and chosen professional ethic through testing of virtues such as trust, loyalty, and integrity.

Specifically, regarding the military profession, with an altruistic theme, Pauline Kaurin writes, "This will require the exercise of judgment about moral claims and commitments; what 'moral' means here is not a person's individual morality but rather ethical norms in the context of military professionalism. Any appeal must be to that standard."[1] Furthermore she claims, "This will require more attention to and education in the exercise of professional judgement and discretion within the ethical frame of military professionalism so that, like other skills and habits of mind essential to the profession this is practiced and well developed." Such defining moments are not fleeting emotional or cognitive experiences. A transformative trusted agent of character from any

[1] Pauline Kaurin, "Professional Disobedience: Loyalty and the Military" by Pauline Shanks Kaurin, Real Clear Defense 08 August 2017," *Real Clear Defense*, August 8, 2017.

profession must experience defining moments throughout life for their own self-preservation, the greater preservation of their ethos, and ultimately for those who are served and benefit by that profession. For any professional, I believe three questions create a framework for character formation and transformational moral leadership of trusted agents.

Who am I as a trusted professional?

Transformational moral leadership springs from an individual's corresponding beliefs and values answering the question, "Who am I as a trusted professional?" What virtues, values, beliefs, education, and experiences forge a leader others can trust? Answering this question requires a self-reflection of being. What grounds a leader of character? How does the essence of being authentic to self, create transparency and authenticity, thereby earning trust with others?

Who are we as a trusted profession?

Ethical leadership answers, "Who are we as a trusted profession?" Ethical leadership emanates from a systemic context and social constructs including code, creed, or ethos requiring individual ethical development. If you are part of a profession providing professional services to clients, you are the face, voice, handshake, and commitment of the company to that client. Professional organizations that I have been part of throughout my life such as the military, scouting, and the church lose the trust of those they desire to serve when immoral autonomous agents who lack character violate the ethos of the profession and break the trust of those who rely upon that profession. In such circumstances, the profession itself must assess what virtues and values it upholds and defends and how it is holding its' professionals accountable. As we seek to understand moral psychology, we consider the philosophical question does a good barrel of apples get contaminated by a bad apple, or does a bad barrel contaminate good apples? Who you are as a trusted professional directly impacts how clients and those seeking to partner with you trust your profession.

Who benefits from us?

The development of trusted professionals within a professional ethic confidently answers a third question, "Who benefits from us, and how?" This question invokes the MBA mantra of people, planet, and profit. Who we are, what we think, and how we lead directly impact those we lead, who we work for, and who we serve internally and externally of our ethos. For much of the twentieth century, profit took precedent over these three. Today that seems to be shifting with a greater emphasis and value on human flourishing and people development and environmental stewardship and compliance.

Moral Philosophy and Ethical Theories

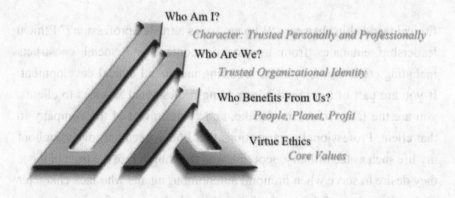

Who Am I?

Character: Trusted Personally and Professionally

Who Are We?

Trusted Organizational Identity

Who Benefits From Us?

People, Planet, Profit

Virtue Ethics

Core Values

Transforming Amateurs to Professionals

These three questions shape the first pillar of the Vanguard XXI Leadership Model of Character. We will add a second set of three questions as we continue in the next chapter, the "3 Q's of Who." Who are you? How do you think morally and ethically? How do you lead?

Transforming amateurs to professionals is a process. It requires practice. More importantly, it requires individuals and organizations to embrace and execute a growth mindset of continual improvement while protecting and not compromising on the non-negotiable virtues and principles that qualify them as trusted moral and ethical leaders of character. Trusted professions are regulated internally by trusted leaders of character and held accountable by those they serve. I'll say it again and again. Ownership drives accountability and accountability drives ownership. You cannot surge character in the moment of crisis. Therefore, how do leaders and organizations of character teach, train, and empower leaders to prepare for those crises to respond appropriately? I believe it results from a life of practicing excellence. It requires diligent pursuit of aligning our passion, purpose, and precision in how we live an excellent life.

As you reflect on this chapter, where are you performing as an amateur where others need a greater professional response? Where are you excelling as a professional leader of character? How are you teaching, training, coaching, and empowering those around you to be accountable and take ownership of their own moral character and the ethos of your profession? How are you taking ownership and holding your organization accountable as a trusted group of professionals? Who is benefiting from what you do, individually and collectively, each day?

··· Chapter Three: The Three Qs of "Who"

"A person's a person, no matter how small." In the Dr. Seuss classic *Horton Hears a Who*, Horton the Elephant's passion, purpose, and precision to save the Whos of Whoville presents a moral imperative for human flourishing. Despite the adversity his fellow animals create for Horton, he remains grounded in who he is, continues to work through a moral and ethical decision-making process on how he will protect and save Whoville. Eventually, he leads the Whos to find their voice, empowering them and himself to gain the trust and support of his adversaries, now turned allies. Who knew a children's book could be so profound? Leaders of character find fulfillment practicing a life of excellence when they pursue a journey of discovering and internalizing who they are, how they think, and how they lead to transform other people's lives.

Every warrior class shares a rich historical narrative describing the ethics, norms, and beliefs that it uses to teach and train warriors. Altruistic virtues—such as courage, wisdom, justice, temperance, faith, hope, love, honor, truthfulness, courtesy, loyalty, sacrifice, and selfless service—

shape both a warrior's ethos and character. Regardless of historical era, eastern or western philosophy, tribal warriors, or a nation state's professional officer corps, these foundational virtues are found in each respective warrior society's culture and religious belief system.[2]

Theological and philosophical concepts shape the warrior profession, a profession that directly impacts the life and death of the human soul and its respective society's ability to flourish. Those who voluntarily choose such a profession bring into it their own character-shaping values and belief systems. They must reconcile their moral worldview with the warrior ethos of their profession, thus creating a life-long learning process of character development and identity formation. The healthy tension of autonomous moral beings operating within a heteronomous ethic necessitates a holistic approach to shaping the character of a warrior and a warrior class. The same goes for any profession and group of professionals pursuing excellence. Shaping high performance people of character, organizations of culture, and climates of excellence embody this ethos. Marketplaces may differ slightly in approach; however, high performing teams are seeking the same outcome. Transformational leaders who can see the world through an epistemological lens regarding human flourishing, critical thinking, and effectively leading diverse teams pursue this relentlessly.

The transactional "sage on the side" is outpaced by the information world, and if not socially aware is out of touch with their audience. Today, audiences have quicker access to information than any "subject matter expert" giving a keynote. I first began to witness this in 2016 as a pastor and ethics instructor. I would say something from the pulpit or classroom podium, or show a slide, and the audience would raise their cell phones, snap a picture, and now, with their heads down and no longer paying attention to me, begin to google more data. Or as Channing Tatum's

---

[2] Shannon French, *The Code of the Warrior* (Maryland: Rowman & Littlefield, 2017).

character, Jimmy Logan, in *Logan Lucky* says, "Yeah, it's a tough one too. I looked it up on the Google."

There is a transformational space for keynote speaking to inspire and impact large audiences with a transformational message, the essential follow-up to a great keynote for me is the leadership development and coaching that transpires for individuals and organizations *after* the fact. So, if I ever have the pleasure of sharing a keynote address with you and your team, please by all means let's have a side stage conversation afterwards on next steps to transform your leaders and organization. The transformational "guide on the side" journeys with people and organizations pursuing excellence empower their unique capital and potential. There are key differences between transactional and transformational leadership. Transactional leadership development and classes are didactic in nature with a sage on the stage talking *at* an audience. Whereas transformational leadership development is different.

This type of leadership is facilitated by a guide on the side, who engages *with* an audience in *their* environment, coaching character, evoking awareness, creating curiosity, and empowering excellence in driving transformative results. Great keynotes facilitate this environment and essential follow-up on growth with intentional leadership development and coaching. Transformational leadership emphasizes human flourishing. Thus, it begins in the soul.

An epistemological approach to identity formation, decision-making, and leadership philosophy implies transformation comes from within the soul, rather than by conforming to secular ideologies. Ah yes, epistemology. Basically, the philosophical study of knowledge and the world around us collectively using the lenses of theology, ethics, science, mathematics, psychology, and history. Or … "the theory of knowledge, especially with regard to its methods, validity, and scope. Epistemology is the investigation of what distinguishes justified belief from opinion." (Online Chrome Dictionary)

The Italian humanists, like Aquinas and Petrarch, brought it back into vogue nearly one thousand years ago. We are losing it again in our world today with radical social, political, and religious agendas demanding people adhere to what to think collectively and no longer how to think critically. This fundamental principal exegetes from Romans 12:1-2, and rightly supports human flourishing through the Creator transforming the creation. It validates the Genesis creation story and affirms the Apostle Paul's statement in Ephesians 2:10, saying we are God's handiwork created to do God's will.

Romans 12:1-2 was one of Dr. Martin Luther King's most powerful sermons titled, "Transformed Non-Conformist."[3] I read it as my devotional every MLK Day. "Do not conform to the pattern of this world but be transformed by the renewing of your mind. Then you will be able to test and approve what God's will is—his good, pleasing, and perfect will." (Romans 12:2, NIV) Dr. Martin Luther King Jr. exemplified living the life of a transformed non-conformist. He preached his aptly titled sermon on several occasions in the fifties and sixties as a pastor, theologian, and peaceful protestor advocating for civil rights.

Multiple versions of this sermon can be found in the public domain today. King's sermon transcends time, being just as applicable today for shaping the character development of trusted moral agents as it was then. In our nation's current social and political turmoil, true moral leadership from transformed non-conformists is necessary amid those masquerading as such. Political operatives and activists across the political spectrum today are attempting to hijack true transformed nonconformists who are engaging in movements that respect and value democratic principles, rule of law, and human flourishing.

King states, "'Do not conform' is difficult advice in a generation when the crowd pressures have unconsciously conditioned our minds and feet to move to the rhythmic drumbeat of the status quo." Today's crowd

[3] Warner, Michael, ed. *American Sermons: The Pilgrims to Martin Luther King Jr*. Third. Vol. American Sermons. New York: The Library of America, 1999.

pressures, many driven by Marxist movements, are intent on destabilizing and destroying America's democratic rule of law through social media platforms, higher education, subversive algorithms and AI, and an uneducated mass of people who numbly follow the latest trending post. Contrary to external crowd pressures, transformed non-conformists must experience transformation from within to promote human flourishing rather than conform to the depraved patterns of the world. King explains, "We are called to be people of conviction, not conformity, of moral nobility, not social respectability. We are commanded to live differently and according to a higher loyalty."

King reminds his audience that the ethic of love modeled by Jesus shines a light on the darkness of the world's conformity to sin. He states that every human being, in the words of Longfellow, must choose to "either be the anvil or the hammer," someone who will either be molded by society or will choose to mold society. Moral agents gain trust, exercising moral autonomy. When they advance the moral and ethical heteronomous ethos, they are part of or make necessary changes to an ethos that has chosen vice over virtue. King's message calls out certain institutions and policies of his time requiring transformation. This included addressing the willingness of the church to conform to majority opinion out of fear of being ostracized for advancing civil rights and ending segregation. He also addressed the dangers, as did President Eisenhower of the Military Industrial Complex. These principled concerns are still applicable, half a century later.

King's theologically grounded message warns potential transformed non-conformists that power or salvation is not found in nonconformity itself. Rather, he again quotes the Apostle Paul and states that morally right transformation begins in the mind by the Spirit of God. King closes his sermon with an admonition that living rightly as a moral agent is difficult and full of peril, but the world needs "men and women who will courageously do battle for truth." Therefore, transformational leadership is necessary and foundational. This style of leadership emanates from an individual's beliefs and values; it is not secular in nature.

Moral leadership answers the question of one's identity as a trusted professional. Ethical leadership emanates from a systemic context and/or social constructs including codes, creeds, or ethos requiring individual ethical development. Ethical leadership answers the question of a group's identity in its role as a trusted profession. Character development is the metaphysical, cognitive, and psychological process of moral and ethical transformational leader development. The development of trusted professionals, within a professional ethic, confidently answers the third question of who benefits from this group and how so. This creates a healthy tension between deontological and utilitarian principles of moral philosophy, where out of a spirit of duty and *a priori* principles, right intent drives right actions to a right end state, while also reinforcing the value of a moral and ethical end state for the greater good.

While transactional leadership may be necessary in maintaining systems and organizational structure, transformational leadership influences human capacity, potential, and flourishing. Thereby teaching morally autonomous trusted agents how to operate within trusted ethical organizations. This holistic approach to character development requires three pillars of transformational moral leadership: moral courage, moral reasoning, and moral empathy.

In short, transformational moral leadership engages, elevates, expands, refines, and forges people of excellence through moral courage, moral reasoning, and moral empathy.[4] I use the word "moral" adjectively with courage, reasoning, and empathy to emphasize the autonomy of human emotion, reason, and volition. Each of us possesses a moral worldview, or how we see the right and wrong in the world according to our own beliefs, education, experiences, values, and virtues. However

---

[4] Some material in this project comes from previous work: Anthony Randall, "Transformational Moral Leadership and the Army Human Dimension Strategy 2015" (Atlanta, GA, Emory University, 2016).

subjective our moral worldviews may be, they are connected to objective truths such as the virtue of courage, logic, reasoning, and the practice of empathy.

Who Am I?

The basic definition of one's identity seems simple. As an Army guy, I always knew to respond with my name, rank, social security number, and date of birth. A well-practiced skill, especially in SERE School. However, when we begin to truly define our identity, we usually reply more holistically. We inherently understand that people receive norms and values from our family heritage, cultural backgrounds, and religious experiences. There is a collective loyalty to our community's, state's, and country's ethos, providing a framework of rules, laws, and consequences to shape personal ideals of right intent, right action, and right outcome.

Personal life experiences round out this list. We also see ourselves through the lens of our psychological personality type. Dr. Carl Jung popularized this study in the twentieth century and his theories today are found in personality type assessments such as the global gold standard, Myers-Briggs Type Indicator (MBTI). One of Dr. Jung's students, Dr. Jolande Jacobi, furthered his work and is found today in the Insights Discovery Model. Jung's work also influenced William Marston's DISC assessment, looking at how personality impacts behavior. Each of these assessments help us to better understand how we see the world, process information, interact with others, and make decisions. These assessments are extremely helpful in helping leaders understand who they are, how they are perceived, and how they can effectively communicate and understand other people. When properly facilitated, these assessments add incredible value to individuals and teams seeking to practice excellence in who they are, how they make decisions, and how they lead.

As a certified Myers Briggs facilitator, the differing MBTI assessments are my go-to, especially the MBTI Conflict Style Report.

Having studied Jungian psychology, I can fully incorporate the Insights and DISC concepts and language into training. Personally, I prefer an ENTJ (Myers Briggs), Id (DISC), and Orange/Red Motivator/Director (Insights) personality type. It's how I see the world, process information, make decisions, lead, and influence others. How about *you*? How does *your* answer to "who am I" begin to change from extrinsic influences to intrinsic virtues, which act as a foundational framework of your character? Maybe you begin to list altruistic virtues found in Western and Eastern philosophies, such as courage, wisdom, justice, temperance, faith, hope, love, honor, truthfulness, courtesy, loyalty, service, and integrity. How do your extrinsically learned norms and values find their foundation in such virtues, and intrinsically transform your character?

Character development, in Aristolean terms of pursuing happiness and excellence, means finding the center or the mean of a virtue, rather than vices of that virtue. Therefore, the question of identity must be asked throughout a leader's life as a moral azimuth check in an amoral world. May I use a military analogy again? Forging the warrior ethos of the American soldier protects the soul of the American soldier from moral injury. Moral injury is a soul wound. Dr. Jonathan Shay describes a moral injury as a "betrayal of 'what's right.'"[5] Character development protects the warrior's soul and psyche, promoting integrity in lieu of fragmentation. Warrior codes protect warriors extrinsically by setting ethical rules, laws, and consequences for behavior. The healthy tension of shaping a warrior's soul intrinsically and extrinsically hopefully prevents "the painful paradox" that fighting for one's country and way of life may result in the inability to live after the fact as a normal citizen.

How does this impact you as a professional in your profession? How do you protect your soul, i.e., the ability to "live with yourself," even when an outcome does not reflect positively on your intent and decision-making process? We all revert to asking ourselves, "who am I?" And, if we remain

---

[5] Jonathan Shay, *Achilles in Vietnam: Combat Trauma and the Undoing of Character* (New York: Simon & Schuster, 1994).

true to who we are, then, regardless of the positive or negative outcome, we are reaffirmed in our character.

Theologically, scripture affirms that our identity comes from being created in the image of God. In the Jewish tradition, Psalm 139:14 reminds us, "We are fearfully and wonderfully made." And like the prophet, Jeremiah, God knew us before we were formed in our mother's womb. (Jeremiah 1:5) That was good news for Jeremiah. After all, he was the weeping prophet. He spoke a great deal of truth and wisdom, however, was seldom positively received by senior leaders. In the Christian tradition, dying to self and living for Christ, creates a spiritually experiential journey of righteousness, clarity, and purpose. Our identity, calling, and election must be sure. Transformational moral leadership affirms these theological truths as essential foundation elements, which lead people to answer fully and truthfully about their own identities. What epistemological lenses help *you* answer the question, "Who am I?"

Who Are We?

Let me ask you a second question. Who are you as a trusted professional within a trusted profession? Every profession has an ethos or a code; it is what separates amateurs from professionals. A military audience may respond with the seven Army Values or the three Marine Corps values, reflecting the altruistic values already mentioned. Each distinct branch of service, and each distinct specialty within those services, have additional exclusive creeds. For example, the Army adheres to the seven Army Values and the Soldier's Creed. Yet, if one desires to become an Army Ranger, the Ranger Creed must be adhered to as well as the virtue of duty to accomplish the mission regardless of cost: "Though I be the lone survivor."[6]

US military officers take an oath to support and defend the Constitution of the United States. This oath is sworn to the ideal of

---

[6] "Ranger Creed," U.S. Army, accessed July 1, 2020,

democracy and rule of law of the Constitution. It is not an oath sworn to an elected leader, political party, or social movement that changes or sways over time. Historically, warrior codes can be written or unwritten. They are exclusively self-regulated, followed, defended, and maintained by those who adhere to the oath, rather than managed by an outside political, social, or religious agency. To adhere to the code is to become a trusted professional. To violate the code is to be deemed a "persona non grata" by fellow code-bearers.

Warrior creeds are familiar to their own cultural belief systems. However, for the warrior and their profession these beliefs are held in higher regard, since their profession carries the weight of decisions that lead to life or death. Research depicts a universal continuity between warrior codes as they are all "closely linked to a culture's religious beliefs and can be connected to elaborate rituals and rites of passage."[7] The warrior and the warrior's code are sacred; character development begins in the soul.

General George C. Marshall wrote, "The soldier's heart, the soldier's spirit, the soldier's soul, are everything. Unless the soldier's soul sustains him, he cannot be relied on and will fail himself and his command and his country in the end."[8] While his quote is directed towards the profession of arms, any profession in our complex world requires a holistic and integrated response, which sees the soul as the origination point for transformational moral leaders. Thus begins a series of choices for any moral autonomous agent who must maintain moral autonomy and yet adhere to a greater professional heteronomy. Through assessment, selection, training, operational experiences, and individual and institutional education, a trusted agent of moral character must assess how to operate as a morally autonomous agent within a greater heteronomous ethos.

---

[7] French, *The Code of the Warrior.*, 4.
[8] "Speech at Trinity College, June 15, 1941," The George C. Marshall Foundation, accessed July 1, 2020, https://www.marshallfoundation.org/library/digital-archive/speech-at-trinity-college/.

To give a visual, imagine two circles converging with one another, like a classic Venn diagram. The more space the two circles have in common, the more likely it is that a leader's passion, purpose, and precision is aligned. However, if those two circles do not have a lot of space in common, this indicates a conflict of interest which creates unhealthy tension. It also likely demonstrates that an individual may seek some other profession, or lacks the maturity to function in any profession, remaining a morally autonomous amateur unable to live by a greater ethos. When this circumstance arises, typically the profession may remove the person, citing that they are "not a good fit."

The COVID pandemic exacerbated this as well. Dubbed, "The Great Resignation," people opted out of organizations they felt no longer aligned with their personal desires, needs, and perspectives. The workforce reexamined their basic, psychological, and professional growth needs and expectations. Towards the tail end of COVID the "Great Remorse" occurred. People began realizing that sitting at home in their pajamas, eating Cheetos and binge-watching Netflix series between Zoom calls, was not as fulfilling as they once hoped. Professionals reflected on the value of being part of value-based, character-driven organizations, where they could add value and have their basic, psychological, and professional growth needs met. Others saw an opportunity to venture out on their own in the "gig" economy having rediscovered their passion, purpose, and precision of what they love to do.

As of this writing, this has created a time of the "Great Recruitment." (Okay, I dubbed this one myself, and it's true.) Professional organizations are in a prime space and place to recruit, assess, select, and acquire high character, high talent trusted agents who are ready to get back in the game. The question organizations must ask moving forward, learning lessons from the last few years, and understanding a changing global workforce and economy is, "who benefits from us?"

Who Benefits from Us?

Consider for a moment that the answer to this question is in fact the extrinsic end state of transformational moral leadership. It hinges upon how a leader answers the first two questions, "who am I?" and, "who are we?" If trusted professionals successfully and intrinsically answer the first two questions, the answer to this third question is clearly that people, the planet, and organizational bottom lines flourish.

Transformational leaders must answer both sets of these six questions accordingly. They are not static in nature; they are dynamic. A new job. A new promotion. New relationships. New responsibilities. Who benefits from you depends upon three additional questions we will address in the following chapters. Who are you as a person of character? How do you critically, morally, and ethically make decisions? How do you lead? These questions are not static in nature. They are not answered once in a classroom or gleaned from a practical experience or two. These questions are fluid for transformational leaders who practice self-reflection, are open to feedback, and are agile leaders with a growth mindset capable of change.

Who benefits from you when they place their trust in you as a professional? That depends how well you practice answering these questions. What more are they expecting, demanding, and holding you accountable for as a professional compared to an amateur? Your profession provides that ethos, those ethical values. Your moral compass provides you the guiding virtues, values, and beliefs that guide you as a moral autonomous leader.

The martial arts demand warriors to honor the profession. For professionals, developing honor requires "determining your obligation," "weighing every situation for justice," and "taking courage and act[ing]."[9] The martial arts demand practice. They demand a white belt mentality to grow and practice at the black belt level of character and skill. I've trained in martial arts since 1988. I'm almost fifty and still get on the mat three to

---

[9] Forrest Morgan, *Living the Martial Way: A Manual for the Way a Modern Warrior Should Think* (New Jersey: Barricade Books, 1992).

four days a week, albeit with a little less speed, strength, and flexibility. However, I do not compromise on the quality of practice. My obligation is to myself and fellow students. What moves I use, and how much force or technique I use, depends upon the level of my opponent. My mindset, regardless of how sore or tired I am, is to maintain a growth mindset and get on the mat.

Transformational leadership demands practice. Those we lead expect us to fulfill our obligation of practicing excellence in character, thought, and action. We are to weigh every situation justly with sound logic, reason, and emotional intelligence. We are to lead with character and courageously act. As my good friend, Command Sergeant Major Walt Zajkowski, a two-time US Army Best Ranger winner and career special operations leader, says "character is your currency" as a leader. When I look back today to twenty-six years ago and reflect on young second lietenant Randall, I am thankful for the leaders who committed to a lifetime of practice long before I did. They highlighted what "not to do," and more importantly, modeled by example that a person of character knows who they are, how they think, and how they lead. Practicing excellence is a process, and trusting this process is a challenge for all of us.

··· Chapter Four: VUCA (Volatility, Uncertainty, Complexity, and Ambiguity)

Practicing a life of excellence must go must deeper than a political affiliation, cultural ethos, or sexual identity. Now, if you consume the daily dosage, or frighteningly more of mainstream media (which I'm not recommending as a practice of excellence), the following depiction of the last twenty years in the United States may sound familiar. It's in your face every day.

After reading a 2021 Pew Research study on political typology, I'm even more disheartened at the divisiveness and lack of civility today in our public square. The study breaks down the following political groups: progressive left, establishment liberals, democratic mainstays, outsider left, stressed sideliners, ambivalent right, populist right, committed conservatives, faith and flag conservatives.[10] I don't know about you but

---

[10] https://www.pewresearch.org/politics/2021/11/09/how-the-political-typology-groups-view-major-issues/

I'm not sure I want to be pigeonholed in any of those categories. Can we have one in the middle that says, "Americans for Human Flourishing?" How do we practice excellence and pursue human flourishing while transforming lives and organizations with so much dissent?

If we are listening to the world around us, and within us ... well you, not me (okay, not you, the person next to you) ... many see a constitutional crisis not seen of this magnitude since the secession of the Confederate States and the American Civil War. Politicians, civil servants, and citizens usurping authority never granted to them by the Constitution. Patriotism or Insurrection? Stolen votes or voter fraud? It depends if you voted blue or red, or have the audacity to vote independently. Some contend it's the same argument over the same votes, just a different year. The judicial courts', including the Supreme Court's neutrality and autonomy to defend the Constitution, are being manipulated to change the Constitution unconstitutionally.

Many citizens are naïve or disinterested; misinformed or overinformed. Uneducated or intellectual derelicts disregarding the very rule of law and spirit of liberty protecting their freedoms. The American Revolution and the founding fathers' classic liberalism and the pursuit of virtue and character are seemingly under attack. Or others believe we just need to scrap it all and write a new Constitution. Does it need to be rewritten or reread? These ideals are politically held sacred across the aisles of Congress, just from different perspectives. Are borders necessary, debatable, or detestable? It depends which side of the fence you are on, and how close you live to one. Are we talking national borders, or the invisibly visible borders in our own communities? Peace! Or Give War a Chance! Is religion an essential and a foundational pillar of our national heritage, family dynamics, and community builder, or a myopic, exclusive, extreme, and bigoted one, especially if it is Christianity or Judaism? Religion is man-made. Hurt people hurt people. "I'm not religious, just spiritual." Whatever that means. Is love an attribute of God? or have we made a new definition of love our god?

Sexual identity and race must be given free choice with a broad spectrum of education and medical services provided to ensure equality. Unless sexual identity and race are objective, scientific, and spiritual truths deconstructed and weaponized by those demanding inclusivity to destroy anyone not subjectively inclusive enough for their liking. Pro-choice? Pro-life? Who decides? The Supreme Course decided once for the nation. Then, changed its mind. And mind you, we are told you can only be happy about one decision. The correct decision, of course. Abolishing law enforcement is legitimate legislation. Racial injustice prevails despite legislation, billons of government dollars and exhaustive social justice movements. Sunday morning church still seems to be the most segregated day of the week. Economics are used to marginalize and oppress communities, instead of assisting and growing them. We give less and we take more. Food deserts abound. Human trafficking is business as normal, and not just for the elite or those in poverty. Fentanyl kills.

Parents and public educators are in a battle for the hearts and minds of America's youth. Focus on the family. Focus on your own damn family! American academic institutions have become a playground for progressivism and the dangerous radicalization of students with philosophical paradigms that sound wildly egalitarian in the confines of a classroom but have proven historically disastrous. You cannot rewrite history. Or can you? College is no longer the best option. Homeschoolers rule. We have an anxious generation addicted to technology, and parents too. Is AI good or evil? Don't worry, it will tell us what to believe. Tik Tok ticks on as I type. Is it a constitutional freedom of speech or a form of foreign espionage and thought control?

If you listen to all of it every day, it's just overwhelming.

What I do believe, philosophically and epistemologically speaking, is that freedom requires a people whose character is rooted in virtue and whose spirit for liberty cannot be extinguished. Nation states require a rule of law, borders, financial security, and national defense. The Magna Carta, Mayflower Compact, Declaration of Independence, Constitution of the

United States and Bill of Rights, while historically progressive in pursuing human flourishing, all fall short of God's commandment to love God and people equally. A document alone cannot preserve freedom.

"Freedom requires limited government, but limited government requires unlimited character in the citizens, the habits of the heart."[11] The Greeks and Romans argued for the place and purpose of virtues in the public and private life. America's founding fathers debated between classic and liberal republicanism and whether virtue alone could sustain freedom. Today, in reflection, Dr. Os Guinness insists that a "golden triangle of liberty" is needed whereby "freedom requires virtue, which requires faith, which requires freedom."

Practicing excellence requires freedom, virtue, and faith.

Freedom in and of itself is its own greatest threat; it requires discipline. Liberty requires law; virtue must be valued; and character must be cultivated. People of faith experience freedom and liberation through spiritual disciplines. High performance athletes win championships by adhering to a disciplined training regimen and teamwork. Highly trusted businesses and institutions retain profit margins and customer loyalty through trusted business ethics.

Our nation requires leaders of character, rooted in altruistic virtues, with a spirit of liberty and a respect for the rule of law. Developing the character of high-performance leaders and organizations embraces Guinness's golden triangle of liberty. Unfortunately, in today's public square, civility is lost, character is questioned, faith is prohibited, and virtue is replaced with emotivism. Ethos erodes in such a space. Practicing excellence through human flourishing and transformational leadership is a process of restoring the public square as a place of collaboration, growth mindset, respect, trust leadership, and opportunity for everyone.

Ethos, Logos, & Pathos Defined

---

[11] Os Guiness, *The Last Call for Liberty: How America's Genius for Freedom Has Become Its Greatest Threat* (Downers Grove, IL: InterVarsity Press, 2018), 118.

Stated simply, ethos, logos, and pathos demonstrate who we are, how we think, and how we lead as influential transformational leaders. They represent our ability to lead and influence via our heart, head, and hands. Aristotle appealed to ethos, logos, and pathos collectively as a form of rhetoric in which to influence people and organizations. Ethos (heart) examines how leaders utilize their character to influence teams. Logos (head) demonstrates how leaders employ logic, reason, and critical thinking to influence processes and people. Pathos (hands) appeals to the emotions and influence of what people do in response to a leader's influence. Today we face a society that is quickly losing the virtue of such rhetoric. People who choose to practice excellence as leaders of character recognize this and implement this rhetoric into their daily practice to positively influence, lead, and transform organizations. So, what are we facing?

Ethos Eroded

This crisis entered my ethics classroom one day when a newly minted West Point second lieutenant stood up and began to list the fallacies of the Constitution and a democratic republic, instead advocating for communism. He lobbied for throwing out Jefferson, Madison, Aristotle, Kant, and Aquinas and replacing their ways with the teachings of Marx and Nietzsche. He later became nationally known for photos taken at his graduation from West Point, as he exposed a Che Guevara t-shirt under his uniform and posed with a closed fist and sign in his hat stating, "Communism will win." Not the best optic for such an institution renowned for cultivating leaders of character.

He was dishonorably discharged from the United States Army, only a few years later, after expressing support and sympathy for foreign governments and violating the Uniform Code of Military Justice for speech against US government leaders. His combat experience in Afghanistan, and his presumed radicalization by a former civilian

Academy professor of Middle East history, attributed to his worldview. The professor was placed on administrative leave and is no longer on the Academy faculty.[12] Today, the now former Army officer is a member of the Democratic Socialists of America.

West Point graduates understandably became deeply disturbed about what kind of moral agents are teaching and training future trusted professionals of character at one of America's most prestigious leadership institutions. Board members, investors, leaders, and alumni of any professional institution rightfully become alarmed when the ethos of their identity, livelihood, and profession is threatened. We still see this trend today with the 2023 Ivy League scandals, antisemitism, progressivism, and a call for reform of our acclaimed academic institutions curriculum and leadership. What happened to these institutions once founded and grounded in teaching and training epistemologically faith, humanities, and liberal arts? How did we forget who we are?

Logos Lost

For the last several years I have served as a guest lecturer on developing a professional ethos and strategic ethical decision-making in a prominent state university's Doctoral Business Administration (DBA) leadership program. The audience is comprised of male and female senior executives and leaders from global corporations, small to medium-sized businesses, and entrepreneurs, as well as several international students. And what I've found over the years is a strong and diverse range of epistemological beliefs. During our facilitation the class typically ask questions regarding professionalism, ethical decision-making, and how an institution of any kind creates a professional code. I was looking forward to another thoughtful interaction one fall semester. Class went well, with excellent class participation, perspective, and dialogue. Until one post graduate student asked what I thought to be an odd question.

---

[12] Jim Laporta, "7 Things You Need to Know about the West Point Communist Saga,"

"When, in your opinion, will the military conduct a coup to overthrow, President Trump? And what is the probability of this happening before the next election?"

I had not brought politics up during the class, so I thought it was an attempt at humor by calling out our broken political system. But I was wrong ... very wrong. The student's question was serious and upon asking it vocally affirmed by at least half of their classmates in a room of roughly twenty post graduate students. I paused to create space for the moment and hold the tension for everyone. I was also considering, epistemologically, how should I respond? Before I could reply, an international student from a prominent Middle Eastern country who was a senior executive at a prominent international financial institution, asked if he could answer.

Well, this is going to get chippy, I thought before giving him the floor.

"You Americans are so stupid," he said. "You don't even understand your own law. You don't even understand or realize the question you are asking him."

I took a deep breath. Yes, this is chippy. It's *more* than chippy ... it's choppy. It's ...

He continued, this time addressing the entire class, saying that Americans did not understand the privilege we have living under a rule of law, such as the US Constitution. Then he methodically painted a very bleak picture and contrasted the way his country of origin operates, leading to oppression, marginalization, and human rights violations. When coups take place, when leaders are deposed, people and possessions disappear. Forever. He stated that the student's question violated the very professional code I upheld as a US military officer, as well as my oath of office to the US Constitution.

And he was right.

You could hear a pin drop ... but not for long. The student who asked the question seemingly blew off their fellow student's perspective, turned their attention back to me, and even more adamantly asked their original question a second time. I paused and asked if they really wanted a probability, percentage, or something on a scale of one to ten. I'm all about giving people options and they wanted a no joke probability. I responded, taking my hand and making a giant "zero" with my thumb and fingers, and said there was a zero percent chance of a coup since the military swears an oath to support and defend the Constitution and serves a rightly elected civilian government.

The US military is a microcosm of American society. It's comprised of a variety of cultural, social, religious, economic, and political beliefs. We are an inclusive, diverse, well-educated, well-disciplined, and highly functioning organization with a global presence. We all volunteered to serve on our own volition for something greater than ourselves. Service members are united under a professional ethos and oaths of office and enlistment after swearing to support and defend the Constitution and its rule of law, rather than a carousel of politicians, social movements, and the rule of man. We are trained to support and defend a heteronomous ethos with moral autonomy as moral agents, maintaining an essential balance of rule of law and the spirit of liberty. As I centered the room back on the issue of professional ethics and decision-making, an ancient quote attributed to Thucydides came to my mind.

"The nation that makes a great distinction between its scholars and its warriors will have its thinking done by cowards and its fighting done by fools."[13] Unfortunately, less than one percent of Americans serve in the military. If more did, maybe we would have a greater understanding of ethos, faith, and trust. Even more unfortunate is based upon the latest military recruitment statistics, less than twenty-five percent of military-aged Americans are even capable of serving under current military requirements.

Educating the American public on the professional ethos which shapes the profession of arms, and the logic and critical thinking required to lead, is essential for proper recruitment and retention of military professionals

---

[13] Karl Marlantes, *What It Is Like to Go to War* (New York: Atlantic Monthly Press, 2011).

and understanding for all citizens about the most well-educated, all volunteer force in the world. We must align, teach, train, and coach the art of following our ethos (passion) with our logos (critical thinking), because they will directly impact our pathos (how we lead). Similarly, outside the military, high performance organizations protect the assessment and selection process of the character of people they onboard and protect the cultural ethos of the organization to facilitate a climate of respect, trust, integrity, collaboration, and growth mindset. You can hire for character and build high performance cultures, or you can hire a bunch of characters who will destroy your culture. The choice is yours.

Problematic Pathos

The military, corporations, higher education, and other bureaucratic organizations rely upon annual, semi-annual, or quarterly certifications in ethics practices for their personnel. Some are found in accessible, scheduled, and certifiable training en masse. If your employer mandated it, you may feel taking one of these courses is simply for optics. Or maybe it's to fulfill an enforced standard by society demanding more accountability from supposed trusted institutions. Many times, it seems a waste of time, checking blocks for the sake of checking blocks. Human Resources, DEI, employee engagement surveys, EQ360s … collectively it all seems overwhelming and unnecessary, especially when leadership doesn't respond with a call to action.

Unfortunately, as many of us experience, taking a course to prohibit or limit immoral or unethical behavior is ineffective if the character of the individuals and culture of the organization do not create a climate which values human flourishing. You cannot change the pathos (hands), or behavior only. You must go to the heart, teaching and training the ethos of character. You must address the head and facilitate a growth mindset. Teaching people how to think critically, i.e., logos, and not what to think by the masses or sheer volume of information. Information is only good for information's sake. It must be analyzed for wisdom, knowledge, and truth. Once that is accomplished, a leader can act on actionable intelligence and lead effectively. However, it all begins and ends with character.

For example, some organizations are overwhelmed with ethics and compliance training. The military's annual 350-1 training and its leaders were confronted by this fact in Dr. Leonard Wong's article "Lying to Ourselves." He highlighted the amount of required compliance training exceeded the amount of time in the training calendar. Doing math in public can be dangerous. Leaders were left with a moral and ethical dilemma. They could choose to report a passing compliance rating knowing all training could not be completed, or they could fail their performance evaluations by not meeting the mandated one hundred percent completion.

Leaders became morally numb, essentially lying to themselves about upholding the esteemed ethics of an organization yet violating them for the sake of self-preservation, performance, compliance, and promotion. [14] Information overruled integrity. This resulted in senior levels of command relaxing the compliance standards of training without resolving the issue of teaching, training, and developing the moral and ethical behaviors, character, culture, and climates of organizations. Transactional leadership is the natural and easy default rather than pursuing transformational processes. Transactional leadership manages systems. Transformational leadership leads people. Practicing excellence is problematic when these two leadership styles are not clearly defined or understood.

A good friend and tenured professor at a top university's business school once asked me to speak on moral and ethical leadership. As we exited the elevator to the floor full of MBA, EMBA, and DBA business students, we were greeted with an extra-large wall banner promoting the school's upcoming "inaugural" ethics conference.

"Who messed up?" I asked the professor.

[14] Leonard Wong and Stephen Gerras, "Lying to Ourselves: Dishonesty in the Army Profession," *Strategic Studies Institute and US Army War College Press*, September 9, 2016.

The professor was surprised that I somehow knew about a discreetly protected moral and ethical leadership crisis within the business school. To their relief, I responded I was not aware of any specific crisis, per se, but organizations don't randomly hold ethics conferences for the sake of good ethics. Organizations typically put on "inaugural" ethics conferences after a major ethics violation occurs. In the military we call this being "right of the boom instead of being left of the boom." Or more crudely, CYA, or "cover your ass." Since then, I have been a guest lecturer on strategic moral and ethical decision-making for one of their classes, and they advocated for a postgraduate ethics curriculum. However, after discussing with the dean of the school, it became clear that there is little interest, and there is still no comprehensive ethical leadership curriculum. The dean considers such a program non-essential for post graduates and ethics to be viewed as primarily an undergraduate focus. Pathos without ethos or logos is a failure in Aristotelian rhetoric, at every level of leadership.

This exposes another equally problematic viewpoint regarding mandatory compliance training. The problem is leaders who dismiss ethics, moral reasoning, and character development trainings as solely necessary at a pedagogical level of education and believe it is no longer necessary at higher levels of leadership. Unfortunately, research and anecdotal studies suggest that ongoing training is in fact necessary. Self-aware leaders of character recognize anyone is susceptible to moral failure. "The greatest crisis in the world today is a crisis of leadership, and the greatest crisis in leadership is a crisis of character."[15]

Clinton Longenecker's article "The Bathsheba Syndrome" reveals and defines the prevalence of how and why leaders morally fail. Longenecker addresses the moral and ethical failures of leaders in the business and political spheres. Referencing 2 Samuel 11 and 12, and King David's systemic string of moral and ethical failures as the king of Israel, Longenecker argues the Bathsheba Syndrome among leaders is rooted in

[15] Dave Kraft, *Leaders Who Last* (Wheaton: Crossway, 2010), 94.

our sin nature. Moral failure is prevalent when moral leaders have
privileged access, an inflated belief in personal ability, control of
resources, and loss of strategic focus.[16] Leaders at any level of leadership
can succumb to this syndrome when in pursuit of cognitive dominance,
realistic training, and institutional agility while neglecting their continued
practice of excellence in who they are as a trusted leader of character.

General David Petraeus spoke at my Ranger School graduation. I
worked on his staff as a young captain when he was a one-star brigadier
general. He visited my special operations unit in Afghanistan in early 2011
to hand out awards for valor to two soldiers. In 2012, the scandal broke
about his affair and unauthorized release of classified documents to Mrs.
Paula Broadwell, a reserve Army officer, fellow West Point Graduate, and
a journalist who wrote *All In*, a book about Petraeus's leadership. I always
held a high degree of respect and appreciation for both as leaders. For
many of us, it was a shocking circumstance of moral and ethical failure by
two well-known and trusted leaders of character. How could this happen?

Resisting And Responding to VUCA With Excellence

Experience demonstrates that moral leaders will fail. No leader is immune
to error due to human depravity. Although created in the imago Dei, we
fall short of God's glory, require his grace, and must pursue a life of
spiritual disciplines, virtue, and excellent practice of our ethos, logos, and
pathos. Accountability drives ownership and ownership drives
accountability. Discipline and obedience are soul saving and life-giving
virtues for anyone who desires to finish well. As I shared in my book,
Practice Makes Permanent, disciplined obedience means "to listen."

The world renown Catholic mystic, Henri J.M. Nouewen writes,
"Christian leaders cannot simply be persons who have well-informed
opinions about the burning issues of our time. Their leadership must be

---

[16] Dean Ludwig and Clinton Longenecker, "The Bathsheba Syndrome: The Ethical Failure of
Successful Leaders," *Journal of Business Ethics* 12 (1993): 265–73.

rooted in the permanent, intimate, relationship with the incarnate word, Jesus, and they need to find there the source for their words, advice, and guidance. Dealing with burning issues without being rooted in a deep personal relationship with God easily leads to divisiveness because, before we know it, our sense of self is caught up in opinion about a given subject. But when we are securely rooted in personal intimacy with the source of life, it will be possible to remain flexible without being relativistic, convinced without being rigid, willing to confront without being offensive, gentle, and forgiving without being soft, and true witnesses without being manipulative."[17]

Transformational moral leadership correspondingly springs from the breast of knowing who we are, how we think, and how we lead through practicing excellence in the public square and providing a holistic approach to reduce moral failure in today's VUCA environment. Practicing the right ethos, logos, and pathos begins with a foundation of virtue ethics and character development to transform the public square through human flourishing. Father Nouwen believed for this type of leadership to be "truly fruitful in the future, a movement from the moral to the mystical is required." It's not as far as a jump as you might think. It will transform your life of practicing excellence.

How would you define *your* ethos?

How would you define *your* logos?

How would you define *your* pathos?

Who and what are *you* listening to?

---

[17] Henri J.M. Nouwen, In the Name of Jesus, A Crossroad Book, 1989

··· Chapter Five: Virtue Ethics in a Virtually Lost Public Square

It happens more frequently than naught. Sometime during a leadership development and coaching course with clients, be it Fortune 100 or 500, small to medium-sized businesses, government or military, college and professional sports, higher education, or private clientele, I have an opportunity, through an epistemological lens, to share how faith and the character of the human soul shape who we are, how we think, and how we lead. Typically, this includes an opportunity to share a perspective through my personal faith journey, or a perspective on liberty, virtue, and freedom.

The corporate or individual responses I receive are overwhelmingly positive, appreciative, and typically lead to deeper discussions with individuals or smaller groups. I probably learned to navigate the pluralistic environments best when working with religious and political leaders of opposing worldviews in the Middle East on combat deployments. Or maybe, my experience working in a pluralistic, organizationally flat, high-performance environment like special operations units. I honed that skill teaching ethics and leadership to American and Allied military officers in a secular classroom as an Army ethics instructor. And finally, as a senior pastor leading a congregation where people, regardless of where they may find themselves on the faith spectrum, could receive God's truth and love in a practical way to live a more excellent life.

Regardless of worldview, people ask me where my courage comes from and how I navigate the public sector with personal faith. People from across the socio-political-religious spectrum typically thank me for the professional space and healthy tension I create for groups to experience leadership development and coaching with candor, civility, dignity, inclusion, trust, and respect. Those words are not exclusive, proprietary, or unique to DEI agendas. They are the outcome of what occurs when human flourishing, founded upon faith, virtue, liberty, and freedom, is empowered in the public square by leaders of character pursuing a more excellent way of life.

"Hey man, you're not too bad for a white dude."

The year from 2015-2016 was tumultuous, both socially and politically. The Ferguson Riots, the Clinton versus Trump presidential election, expanding wars in Syria and Ukraine fueled by ISIS and authoritarian regimes led by men like Assad and Putin created college campus tinder boxes. I was a graduate student at Emory University working on a graduate degree in ethics and philosophy. Specifically, I was writing my initial thesis on transformational moral leadership.

I was humbled and honored that my thesis advisor, Dr. Robert Franklin, was a preeminent transformational moral leadership scholar. Dr. Franklin still serves as the James T. and Berta R. Laney Chair in Moral Leadership at Emory's Candler School of Theology. He was the tenth President of Morehouse College and ran for Georgia's Fifth Congressional District following the death of Congressman John Lewis in 2020. Dr. Franklin's work and servant leadership in social ethics and transformational moral leadership inspired me and I am forever grateful to his mentorship and thesis advisement to this day.

While Dr. Franklin and I both love God and people, and share a love for moral leadership, politically speaking, we are "across the aisle" from one another. We have shared many good laughs, and even better conversations. At my request, he graciously endorsed my previous book, and this one too! Despite our differing political opinions, he asked me if I would join his congressional campaign. Unfortunately, I could not as an active-duty military officer, but would have otherwise. In the public square, Dr. Franklin and I, from similar and opposing lenses, desire a public square of human flourishing founded in faith, liberty, virtue, and freedom for all.

His transformational moral leadership class was highly sought after and well attended by a diverse group of students across the socio, political and religious spectrum of Emory University. Being a white, straight, married with kids, active-duty military, ordained minister clearly made me outnumbered by all other affinity groups in the room. Our classroom conversations and debates were beyond colorful. I was even compelled to consider comedian Bill Maher a serious moral leader. In retrospect, almost a decade later, my concurrence and respect for his moral courage grows stronger with every monologue.

I sat at the front of the room, listened patiently to the subjective viewpoints of my classmates, some well founded in epistemological thought, and unfortunately, many opinions scraped a thin line of intellect capable of only emotivism and subjective opinion substantiate by quoting Wikipedia or a Facebook post. Our premier academic institutions have seemingly created an environment void of or lost the ability to teach people how to think epistemologically and critically.

One evening, the conversation became incredibly heated. People were agitated. Emotions led the debate, body language postured for position, tone of voice attempted to control and silence any in opposition to another's perspective. Dr. Franklin always did an excellent job of creating and holding tension in an intellectual space. I took notes and did not actively engage in the debate, as I processed the implications of what I would say and when I would say it. I was keenly aware of safe spaces, emotionally triggered students, and accusing people of micro-aggressions being all the rage.

Eventually Dr. Franklin engaged me, curious about my thoughts and perspective on the issues at hand. Pulling from Greek philosophy and Pauline theology, I pursued a Socratic and epistemological approach, asking questions and seeking clarification, highlighting objective truths and calling into question the validity of subjective statements made. It was too much for some to bear. Outrage! How could I, being who I was, or at least, who I appeared to be through others cognitive bias, dare challenge statements being made in the classroom? Fortunately, we took a well-timed fifteen-minute break.

I went to fill up my water bottle, and while I was at the fountain, three Black male classmates circled around me, their body language saying the conversation wasn't over. I gave them a head nod as they nervously looked around to ensure no one else was listening. Then one of them, seemingly speaking for the group as their heads nodded in agreement, said that I had some real courage to say what I just said in class. And here's the kicker. They made it a point to tell me that they agreed with me, but were afraid to speak up in class. Why? Because if they displayed any level of agreement with me, their own affinity and social groups would ostracize them for their beliefs. I thanked them for their candor and we all agreed to get dinner afterwards. Before they walked away, one of them wrapped up our water cooler conversation saying, "Hey man, you're not too bad for a white dude." We all laughed, hugged, and shook hands, like brothers in Christ should, and spent more lunches and dinners together that year growing together as transformational moral leaders in the public square.

Racism isn't a skin issue, it's a *sin* issue.

As is any -ism that rejects human flourishing. Unfortunately, Sunday mornings are one of the most segregated days of the week ... and we Christians need to change that.

Human Flourishing Starts with the Character of the Heart

What they didn't know was amid the Ferguson Riots and a politically divisive and toxic culture, I supported a fellow Black chaplain to find a location for his Sunday chapel service when their chapel building was closed for renovations. And his chapel service looks a lot like any HBC or AME Sunday gospel service in your hometown. No other chapel congregation would negotiate times or service locations to help them out, even though they could. Even the senior chaplain (a white guy), who oversaw all religious support for service members and families on the military post, told him to go figure it out himself. Fortunately, he was fired a few months later for toxic leadership.

So, the two of us, who affectionately called each other "brother," ate lunch every Wednesday together, and encouraged one another, cast vision together, and came up with a plan to combine our non-denominational chapel service, and at the time one of the largest in the Army, with their thriving gospel chapel service. Altogether, over five hundred military service members and their families were going to become stretched in their faith practice. His deacon board and our leadership council were shocked and apprehensive, yet because they trusted us as leaders of character, they remained curious and open to the idea.

The first Sunday was awesome. Our combined worship teams led the congregation in worship. And the two of us facilitated "team preaching," where we shared a message together sitting on the stage in rocking chairs side by side. Black folks found out white folks can't clap on the right beat, and white folks found out Black folks sometimes run around with banners and flags while singing. It was glorious! When we convened our deacon and leadership teams the following week, they had one question. "When are we going to do this again, and for how long?"

Amid our country's divisive political, religious, and social public square, we found a place for the human soul to flourish. We worshipped together for a few more Sundays. It was joyful, collaborative, and challenging. Although we loved the idea, our congregations appreciated their unique methods of worship and wanted to maintain those distinctions. Unable to move our time earlier because we shared the chapel with our Catholic brothers and sisters for their mass, the gospel service eventually chose to hold their service after ours in the afternoon. Then something happened: our congregation members began attending their services and their congregation members attended ours. We would preach for each other when the other was out of town. Sometimes we would just do it to give our congregations something different. For the following three years, our congregations celebrated Easter Sunday, Christmas Eve, Watch Night, and a summer outdoor baptism and barbeque service together.

My chaplain brother and I both moved on five years ago, and as the military goes, so have our congregations. However, those two chapel services were transformed. To this day, with new congregants and chaplains, those two congregations still come together for church events during the year. I haven't even mentioned holding chapel service for several years running in the Oktoberfest Beer Tent for one of the largest Oktoberfests in the southeastern region of the United States! That is still happening today, half a decade after my departure. What is needed? A change in the character of peoples' hearts. What would it look like if the public square experienced a character of the heart transformation?

Thought Leaders Influentially Leading in the Public Square

This is my wheelhouse; I thrive in a pluralistic public square. Navigating and protecting today's public square requires understanding how what we and others believe interact within our psychological moral development and social constructs. An understanding that offers people an arena with space to grapple with difficult issues in a dignified and respectful way, to a point where we can learn from one another. Grappling epistemologically with issues of how best to initiate, facilitate, and promote human flourishing within our unique local, national, and global cultures and societies. The concept and definition of human flourishing has taken many forms within philosophy. The popularity of promoting human flourishing in the public square, through a Christological view, has ebbed and flowed throughout history ... some good, some bad. Religion can really screw things up because humans made religion. But God made something greater; something religious liberty is supposed to pursue.

Exercising faith in the public square achieves an Aristotelian means of human flourishing in lieu of the feared vice of deficiency, a total exclusion of all religion, or the vice of excess, religious totalitarianism.[18] Yale theologian, Miroslav Volf, adamantly advocates for religious liberty, which may stem from his childhood in a communist bloc country where he witnessed his family members face extreme oppression and persecution. Volf contrasts his position with Sayyid Qutb's Islamic religious totalitarianism, and today's progressive agenda of secular exclusion of religious beliefs in the public square, and in between the two, H. Richard Niebuhr's five classic Christian positions in engaging culture found in *Christ and Culture*. Here, he outlines six points of how the Christian faith may interact with culture in the public square, contrary to the malfunctions of extremist faith and progressive secularism. Christians interact by faith through the inclusive truth and love of God's word, just as Jesus Christ came into the world with grace and peace to free humanity from oppression and coercion.[19] That's not religion. That's faith in something bigger than ourselves.

These ascending elements empower Christians to lead lives of flourishing and aiding others to flourish. It rejects a binary belief, choosing

---

[18] Miroslav Volf, *A Public Faith: How Followers of Christ Should Serve the Common Good* (Grand Rapids: Brazos Press, 2011), ix-xvii.
[19] Ibid., xv-xvi.

instead a "complex attitude" of "accepting, rejecting, learning from, transforming, and subverting" elements of a constantly changing culture. Finally, Volf writes that Christians, while rightfully holding their exclusive religious views, should also serve as the greatest advocates for plurality in the public square. Let me repeat that, especially for my fellow Christians. *Christians, while rightfully holding their exclusive religious views, should also serve as the greatest advocates for plurality.* The Great Commandment to love God and love people is, in reality, the greatest public statement of human flourishing. The altruism of pursuing excellence in a higher power because we are not perfect, and pursuing excellence in our own imperfect society, should resonate with any public square. It's what high performers know to be true about practicing excellence; to strive for perfection while not demanding it. A love for God and people is essential to human flourishing, and essential to human flourishing is a loving and just God. Being relevant outside of Sunday morning without falling complicit to a social gospel is the Church's greatest challenge. So, what's stopping us?

Volf identifies two major malfunctions of faith as idleness, which can lead to secular exclusion from the public square, or coerciveness, which can lead to religious totalitarianism. His solution redefines human flourishing, which "consists in love of God and neighbor and enjoyment of both."[20] He advocates for Christians to "explicate God's relation to human flourishing," to "make plausible the claim" that the Great Commandment is the key to human flourishing, and to faithfully "believe that God is fundamental to human flourishing."

History reveals that when the human soul cannot practice faith, and religion is excluded from public life, a better society has proven false. Instead, liberal democracy and classic republicanism has demonstrated an ideal environment for religious diversity in the public square, where every human soul can find and exercise their voice. It's the reason it's clearly stated in the first amendment of the US Constitution.

---

[20] Volf, *A Public Faith: How Followers of Christ Should Serve the Common Good.*

Volf encourages belief in a character and leadership development curriculum that contains exclusive truth claims promoting human flourishing for love of God and love of neighbor. It should encompass the spiritual, cognitive, and emotional components of every human being. It is imperative to advocate for classic liberalism in teaching and training trusted moral agents of character to exercise moral autonomy within a heteronomous professional ethos. Trusted moral agents responsible for human flourishing must reject a progressive secularism that militantly expunges religion and spirituality for a myopic epistemological gnostic rationalism, while simultaneously rejecting a religious totalitarianism of exclusivity. Both methodologies reject the freedom of the human soul and are not suitable for a civil public square.

So how do we teach and train virtue ethics and character through leadership development and coaching? Let's ask Aristotle.

Virtue Ethics, Character & Drawing Circles

Aristotle's comprehensive work on virtue ethics provides an ancient foundation to character development. He writes, "The agent also must be in a certain condition when he does them (acts) … his action must proceed from a firm and unchangeable character."[21] His ten concise books demonstrate that those who habitually live out the cardinal virtues experience human flourishing as an active and contemplative lifestyle in pursuit of true happiness. We do this by practicing excellence and permanence as a leader of character. A moral agent forms his or her character through habit, "ethike," which is derived from the word "ethos." Aristotle's pursuit of moral and intellectual virtue, and the subsequent habits necessary to achieve such virtue, dives deep into the question of human flourishing and the purpose of human goodness. His idea of pursuing true happiness seeks the virtuous mean rather than the deficiency or excess of a virtue's opposing vices. Moral and intellectual virtues are

---

[21] Aristotle, *Nicomachean Ethics*, 28.

acquired through the right repetition and experiences of reasoning to choose what is noble, advantageous, and pleasant over corresponding vices of what is base, injurious, and painful. For Aristotle, a moral agent experiences human flourishing when "pleasure in doing virtuous acts is a sign that the virtuous disposition has been acquired; a variety of considerations show the essential connection of moral virtue with pleasure and pain."[22]

Theologically, the virtuous believer experiences happiness through the spiritual fruit of joy. The Apostle Paul, an ardent student of Greek philosophy, integrates Aristotle's moral and intellectual virtue throughout his letters to the early church. Joy is found in suffering, according to Paul and James.[23] Character is habitually formed through facing adversity and faithfully believing that experiences and reasoning produce fortitude, character, and hope. Aristotle and Paul emphasize that experience and reason should lead people to what is good, noble, and just, with the warning that this is not easy due to external adversity, persecution, and suffering in the world as well as internal vices in our minds, bodies, and souls. Therefore, true freedom to act requires a virtue to guide those actions, along with the liberty to exercise them through faith, which is the source of those virtues.

Virtue, Vice, and Living a More Excellent Way

Western civilization's "Cardinal Virtues" stem from rediscovering Greek philosophy and Italian Humanism, specifically Plato, Aristotle, and the latter, Thomas Aquinas. There is a familiar saying that for every virtue there is a vice. Mine is a fine cigar and two neat fingers of bourbon. However, that does not explain the full explanation of virtues, or the extent of my bourbon collection and old-fashioned recipes.

---

[22] Aristotle., 25.
[23] See Romans 5:1-5, Galatians 5:22, Philippians 4:4-9 and James 1:1-7.

Every virtue consists of two vices, one of deficiency and one of excess. The challenge in living a more excellent life is pursuing the "mean" of the virtue as Aristotle would explain, thereby avoiding a deficiency or excess in the practice thereof. For example, wisdom, along with courage, is the virtue of the academic according to Plato. Courage is the virtue of the warrior. Justice is the virtue of the politician. Temperance is a virtue required to exercise the other three with prudence and excellence. Wisdom's vices are experienced as foolishness and arrogance. Courage exercised with excellence avoids cowardice and recklessness. Justice, practiced justly, prevents anarchy and oppression. Temperance, well managed, prevents rage and passivity.

Upon the rediscovery of the Greek virtues, Aquinas added three integral theological virtues essential to flourishing of the human soul. Faith, hope, and love. Comically, I call these the "Wedding Crasher" virtues, if you recall the iconic movie *Wedding Crashers,* when Vince Vaughn and Owen Wilson's wedding crashing characters make a side bet during a wedding about whether the pastor uses the famous wedding scripture, 1 Corinthians 13:13. (For the record, as a pastor, I prefer John 2, Jesus' first miracle, out of love at a wedding turned water to wine. Therefore, bourbon may be a vice, but a glass of wine may receive a better classification in practice. Just saying.) Building upon wisdom, courage, justice, and temperance, the human soul thrives by pursuing hope and subsequently dies with the vices of hopelessness and false hope. Likewise, a strong faith looks entirely different than lacking faith (faithless) and the exercise of blind faith, a dangerous excess.

Virtue, Values, Veritas

VICE OF DEFICIENCY	VIRTUE	VICE OF EXCESS
Cowardice	COURAGE	Recklessness
Foolishness	WISDOM	Arrogance
Anarchy	JUSTICE	Oppression
Rage	TEMPERANCE	Passivity
Faithless	FAITH	Blind Faith
Hopeless	HOPE	False Hope
Hate	LOVE	Lust

Finally ... there is love. Aquinas chose a deeper approach than a wedding side bet. He chose a sure thing. The greatest virtue to pursuing a more excellent way of life is love. The Apostle Paul's letter to the Corinthian church, immersed in the pluralistic and morally subjective culture of first century A.D. Corinth sought to encourage those of faith, that in the depth of who they are, how they think, and how they lead, a virtuous and practiced love of God and our fellow human being is foundational. C.S. Lewis, the twentieth century author, philosopher, apologist, and theologian wrote an incredible book titled *The Four Loves*, in which he distinguishes the four types of love we experience as human beings: storge, a love of life or common bond; philia, a love of friendship; eros, an intimate love; and agape, unconditional love for one another.[24] Paul uses the word "agape" to describe the type of love we must pursue as a virtue to live a more excellent life. When we learn to practice all four types with excellence and temperance, we find that of all the virtues the greatest is love.

Paul challenges his readers, then and now, that love is practiced and developed over time. "When I was a child, I spoke like a child, I thought like a child, I reasoned like a child. When I became a man, I put aside childish things." (CSB, I Corinthians 13:11) When we pursue a more excellent life and a virtuous way of living, we put on our big boy and big girl pants, choose a growth mindset, self-regulate (temperance), and look through the lens of the seven virtues in our daily life and practice.

Drawing Circles and Finding the Center: A More Excellent Way

I utilize one of Aristotle's most poignant quotes as a teaching exercise to make the point. I've conducted this exercise with over fifteen thousand people in rooms of a couple dozen to several hundred. The results are always the same. Here's how it plays out: after a thorough discussion on what it means to be a professional and understanding who you are, how

---

[24] C.S. Lewis, *The Four Loves*

you make decisions, and how you lead, I ask students to draw a circle on a blank sheet of paper and find the center of the circle to the best of their ability using all resources available, to include their wisdom, knowledge, and understanding.

Once complete, the students share their methodology with fellow students in small groups before returning to the larger group. In the larger group, I explain that moral autonomy, operating out of our personal moral belief of right or wrong, is much like the circle exercise. Although given the same simple and exact instructions, everyone draws the circle and finds the center differently, based upon their own volition and worldview. Some draw a circle freehand, many of which are not closed, have tails, or look more oval shaped. Others draw the smallest circle possible, to be exact. A third group uses some kind of tool or resource to draw a more exact circle with a coin, ring, bottle cap, or by using grid squares and lines on their paper. When finding the center of the circle, some students mark an indiscriminate "x," crosshairs, a dot, or a smaller circle. Others use a piece of string, ruler, or fold their paper to find a more exact center.

Then, I take a poll to see who drew the circle and found the center without any prior knowledge or use of resources in comparison to those who did, demonstrating a simple form of ethical heteronomy. So, who uses their moral autonomy within the confines of ethical principles of drawing a circle, such as geometry? Only fifteen to twenty percent of participants use a priori principles and available resources to accomplish the task. The majority draw their circle freehand.

After this, I ask two questions demonstrating the point of tension between moral autonomy and ethical heteronomy. How many have been students or teachers of mathematics? How many have studied the ethic, and its corresponding laws, rules, and theorems of geometry of how to draw a circle and find its center? Unanimously, in post high school audiences, everyone answers that they have been a student or teacher in the profession of math, and within that profession have studied the geometrical principles of drawing a circle and finding the center. Yet, when asked to accomplish the task on the spot, only fifteen to twenty percent (typically higher for an audience of engineers) rely upon those ethics. The lesson is that even though trusted professionals have a set of morals and ethics, when put to the common task of applying them, the majority may not intuitively or intentionally apply them at all. This illustrates the competing principles of Kantian deontological reasoning and Hume's non-cognitive approach of how intuition and emotion drive decision-making processes over logic and reason.

Professionals and Amateurs

Several years ago, I was teaching one hundred and twenty Army officer candidates. These are well-educated civilians and enlisted soldiers with undergraduate and graduate degrees who choose to change careers by transitioning to become an Army officer. Following their basic training course, they go through a twelve-week Officer Candidate School (OCS) before commissioning as second lieutenants. It is the largest officer commissioning source in the Army, even more than ROTC and West Point. I asked two OCS students sitting next to each other how they drew their circles. One candidate replied.

"I used a protractor and compass!"

I paused. I was pretty sure protractors and compasses weren't on the OCS packing list. I asked him if those were his tools.

"No, I borrowed them from my battle buddy," he said.

I looked over to his battle buddy and asked him how he drew his circle. Did he use his own protractor and compass as well?

"No, sir. I did not," came his reply.

While I complimented him on sharing his tools with those around him to enhance their success, I was perplexed as to why he did not use the very same tools to enhance his own success.

"How did you draw your circle and find the center, OC?" I asked.

"Sir, I drew it like any normal person would," was his answer.

My jaw dropped, as I was speechless ... and then I smiled. His simple response galvanized the application of the exercise. The process of becoming a civilian to a professional soldier is intentional. Your freedoms are taken away and given back to you as privileges. You are taught to think morally from your own priori virtues and moral worldview, meanwhile within the context of a larger ethic or ethos you have chosen to align with for the greater good, i.e., the profession of arms, the Army, and the Army values. It is through this transition, in any profession, a leader of character must recognize that once they choose to call themselves a professional and uphold the professional ethos, they forfeit the right to live as "any normal person would" and must now practice excellence morally and ethically. The very trust they earn from within their profession, and outside of it, comes from who they are, how they think, and what they do. The benefit received by those they serve depends upon their integrity to live morally and ethically sound lives.

The class ended with Aristotle's quote displayed on the screen and in our coaching workbook, "For in everything it is no easy task to find the middle, e.g. to find the middle of a circle is not for everyone but for him who knows; so, too, anyone can get angry—that is easy—or give or spend money; but to do this to the right person, to the right extent, at the right time, with the right motive, and in the right way, that is not for everyone, nor is it easy; wherefore goodness is both rare and laudable and noble."[25]

The quote emphasizes the difficulty of pursuing a virtuous life as a trusted agent of moral character. It emphasizes pursuing the mean, or virtuous acts, habits, and outcomes, over the fringe vice outliers of excess and deficiency when pursuing the good of human flourishing and happiness. Always a challenge in the public square, which is why not everyone does it. It's why pursuing a more excellent way, practicing permanence and not perfection gives us passion, purpose, and precision in who we are, what we think, and how we lead. From a secular perspective it is about getting one tenth of one percent better every day. Aristotle's

---

[25] Aristotle, *Nicomachean Ethics*, 36.

work provides an essential framework for challenging trusted agents of character to pursue the mean of excellence in life. It is *not* easy, which is why trusted professionals of character are held in high regard.

PE: Draw a Circle. Find the Center.

"For in everything it is no easy task to find the middle, e.g. to find the middle of a circle is not for everyone but for him who knows; so, too, anyone can get angry – that is easy – or give or spend money; but to do this to the right person, to the right extent, at the right time, with the right motive, and in the right way, that is not for everyone, nor is it easy; wherefore goodness is both rare and laudable and noble."
Aristotle, Nicomachean Ethics, Book 2 Chapter 9

From a theological perspective, it's about recognizing we cannot achieve a more excellent way without trusting God in transforming our lives; a process called sanctification. It requires faith, hope, love, and courage to pursue a wise, just, and patient God. And if Paul is correct, which I'll wager he is, it requires us using wisdom to experience receiving and giving God's love with our fellow man.

... PART II: Logos

Moral & Ethical Decision

Making

··· Chapter Six: Beach Jiu-Jitsu &

Practicing Excellence

One of my favorite photos is of Master Helio Gracie teaching presumably his future world champion Brazilian jiu-jitsu sons on a beach. Gracie is standing in an athletic coaching stance, his muscular frame gleaning in the sun, wearing only swim trunks. The boys are roughly six and eight years old and are locked into one another's grips, attempting the classic judo throw, Osoto Gari. Gracie is focused; his hands and body language create an imaginary ring or mat for the boys to move about on the sandy beach.

One boy attempts to throw the other off balance, hands gripping his opponent's arms, as his leg passes by his opponents for the reaping action that will complete the sweep. My hunch is this was not the first time these boys have attempted this throw. Nor is it the first time Gracie has coached them in the process. A good coach creates space for their client to be curious, explore, investigate, and come to their own conclusions. Simultaneously introducing proven techniques, processes, and ethos into the process required for individual and organizational success.

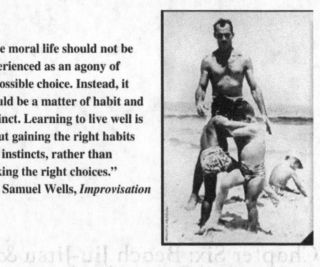

"The moral life should not be
experienced as an agony of
impossible choice. Instead, it
should be a matter of habit and
instinct. Learning to live well is
about gaining the right habits
and instincts, rather than
making the right choices."
   - Samuel Wells, *Improvisation*

Jiu-jitsu is a beautiful martial art, a way of living an excellent life, that requires deliberate practice. Just when a white belt feels they have mastered their space with an opponent, they may be introduced to what blue belt spacing looks and feels like. Over time, a practitioner learns through thousands of hours of practice the slight differences between purple belt and brown belt space, and finally black belt space. A jiu-jitsu player learns and masters a series of moves and positions, identifying which ones work best for their physical ability, flexibility, strength, and skill. This is commonly referred to as "their game."

Jiu-jitsu is an art and science. Rules and principles are respected and followed as one embraces the ethos of community and success on the mat. Within this ethos, each player develops "their game," which many times features similarities of their primary instructor or family line of jiu-jitsu. Jiu-jitsu has its' own epistemology of throws, passes, chokes, locks, submissions, defense, and offense. A well-rounded jiu-jitsu player is epistemologically sound implementing certain aspects of these areas into their game with excellence. This cannot all be taught or absorbed at once, or rigidly adhered to on a predetermined schedule or pace. Each student is different. I'm reminded of the adage, "when the student is ready, the teacher will appear." The teacher, be it a person or experience, may always be present. However, the learning and application occurs when the student comes to the awareness of the presence through their psychological moral development and acquisition of wisdom, knowledge, and understanding.

When speaking in relation to high performance leaders and growth, jiu-jitsu provides a perfect analogy. White belts typically experience large jumps in development and growth over two to three years. Blue belts continue to experience significant gains in skill and technique over the next two to four years. However, once a practitioner reaches purple and brown belt, the gains become smaller and more precise. Although the gains are smaller, they become more consistent—a steady path to mastery—doing "this much," and over another four to six years achieving the rank of black belt. Achieving a black belt in Brazilian jiu-jitsu is typically a ten plus year process. Ninety percent of people who begin BJJ never make it to blue belt, and the percentage to purple, brown, and black belt is a significant drop off.

Practicing excellence is a journey requiring an epistemological approach. Wisdom is the pursuit of virtuous living. It is a deepening of the soul. Knowledge is the cognitive processing of wisdom, organizing, categorizing, and synthesizing how wisdom should be applied to critical thinking. Understanding applies wisdom and knowledge through practical application, exercise, and repetition. It's called praxis.

Creating space for leaders to learn how to make moral and ethical decisions personally and professionally is essential. Building high performing cultures consisting of autonomous trusted moral and ethical leaders of character empowered to make decisions requires leaders who know how to create space in a VUCA world. What's required? Being transformed through practicing an epistemological approach to the art and science of leadership. Yes, epistemological, a big word that once we explore together may become one of your lexicon favorites. We are beginning a deep dive into deeper thinking, so … stand up, stretch, drink some water, and let's go.

An Epistemological Pathway

The Merriam Webster Dictionary defines epistemology as, "the study or a theory of the nature and grounds of knowledge especially with reference to its limits and validity." Epistemological thinking uses a myriad of philosophical paradigms and methods to bring a holistic clarity to the world identifying, justifying, and applying believed objective truths from emotive, unsubstantiated, and syncretistic opinion. Building upon this epistemological approach, how can we explore pursuing a life of excellence through theological, historical, philosophical, psychological, neuroscientific, and experiential truths? Finishing well requires intentional practice. Wisdom (who I am), knowledge (how I think), and understanding (how I lead) leads to successfully navigating our trepidatious world. Wisdom is the first step.

Wisdom is a Virtue, A Love of Knowing God

How does a "theological foundation for character development address striving for moral goodness?" In William Mattison's book, *Introduction to Moral Theology*, he emphasizes the need "to enable people to understand and utilize their practical reasoning better so as to live more virtuous lives.[26]" Moral philosopher Samuel Wells states in his book, *Improvisation*, "The moral life should not be experienced as an agony of impossible choice. Instead, it should be a matter of habit and instinct. Learning to live well is about gaining the right habits and instincts, rather than making the right choices."[27] Therefore, considering philosophical and theological lenses, how do we teach, train, and coach living an excellent life of habit and instinct that naturally embraces practical reasoning and right intent?

---

[26] William Mattison, *Introducing Moral Theology: True Happiness and the Virtues* (Grand Rapids: Brazos Press, 2008).

[27] Samuel Wells, *Improvisation: The Drama of Christian Ethics* (Grand Rapids, Michigan: Brazos Press, 2004). 75

Mattison highlights, "Augustine's argument of the restless human heart's desire for contentment, happiness, and pursuing the excellence of a life well lived. Using Plato's famous interaction between Glaucon and Socrates in *The Republic*, Mattison presents two types of morality: one of obligation and one of happiness.[28] The argument for morality of obligation, represented by Glaucon, seeks the end over the means. People find happiness in getting whatever they want. However, in doing so, irreparable damage may be done to others. Therefore, a morality of obligation is necessary to include adherence to moral norms and laws under such virtues as justice. Happiness is adhering to external norms and laws for the greater good of everyone. Therefore, a heteronomous ethic is shaping the moral agent's reasoning, and actions within that ethos is essential to character development.

Conversely, Socrates argues for a morality of happiness, one of virtuous intention meaning that by living a life of virtue, one finds true happiness in their intent, reasoning, and actions. Even if an individual had the power and position to reject such virtues as fortitude, wisdom, justice, and temperance, they would still choose a morality of happiness by pursuing the means over the ends. The end state of happiness and excellence is found in living a virtuous life. A morally autonomous trusted agent of character who adopts this approach inspires other moral agents to seek lives well lived. Additionally, such moral agents establish, defend, challenge, and correct the heteronomous ethos, ensuring a healthy tension between a morality of obligation and happiness. In sum, finishing well is not about the finish line. It's about the daily practice of excellence that propels a person of character to cross the finish line. Practice makes permanent, practice does not make perfect.

Theologically, my Christians faith prioritize a morality of happiness over a morality of obligation, thereby acknowledging natural law and the necessity of salvific grace. Plato and Aristotle's cardinal virtues of fortitude, prudence, justice, and temperance are considered foundational

---

[28] Mattison, *Introducing Moral Theology: True Happiness and the Virtues.*, 24.

virtues establishing the delicate balance between right intention and the freedom to act. Mattison refers to these "inner-worldly (cardinal)" virtues having "transitive (external)" effects in our world and "intransitive (internal)" effects upon our own moral happiness.

However, unlike the atomism of Epicureanism and the rationalism of the Stoics and Kant, moral theology requires the Pauline and Aquinian theological virtues of faith, hope, and charity (love) to complete the fullness of the cardinal virtues. The theological virtues provide the necessary intentions, reasoning, actions, and worldview that resolves Augustine's concern for the restless heart and sets apart a life well lived through grace from a life well lived by obligation to natural law alone. Therefore, if we are practicing an epistemological approach to character development, it seems moral theology is essential to holistic character development of trusted professionals. The faith, hope, and love exhibited by God, and found in those who pursue God, enable moral and ethical leaders to find joy and fulfillment personally and to experience God's essence of human flourishing.

In beach jiu-jitsu terminology, you learn by habit and instinct to love practicing judo throws on the beach with your training partner and coach, even though the ring may be undefined, the footing unstable, and the sand rubs, grinds, and gets in all the most uncomfortable places. It is good for the soul and promotes confidence to act courageously in any circumstance.

Establishing that foundation, let's move on to courage. Courage, the virtue of the warrior, according to Plato is an extension of such wisdom.

The Code and Courage of the Warrior

Dr. Shannon French spent eleven years as a professor at the United States Naval Academy investigating the warrior ethos and teaching students how to define warrior and warrior code. Her insightful book, *The Code of the Warrior*, is rooted in those pivotal years of training future Naval and Marine officers. She began each semester with a short suspense in-class assignment for students to identify five words synonymous with the word warrior. She offered "murderer," "killer," "fighter," "victor," and "conqueror."[29] She wrote that her students overwhelmingly rejected all five words because authentic warriors adhere to a moral superiority found in a warrior code that transcends any of the proposed synonyms.

Aligning the words "warriors" and "murderers" was the most intensely refuted of the five words. French claimed her students took offense to the term "murderer" because it violates a universal moral virtue of the valuation of life and the divine hand upon life found in every major religion. She challenges her audience through assessing warrior codes across history and cultures to examine what truly defines a warrior code.

Shannon and I have had the privilege of working with one another over the years and collaborated at international and military ethics conferences. Her works continue to provide a proverbial jiu-jitsu ring of boundaries for warriors to execute just acts of war with courage, wisdom, justice, and temperance. They also challenge civilians to carefully consider the concept of human flourishing, how culture shapes a society's warrior ethos, and the moral responsibility a warrior class, or profession of arms, has to the rule of law, their civilian leadership, and citizen counterparts they defend.

Warrior codes are not necessarily systematic, with a set list of rules and regulations. Some may be unwritten, yet found in a people's songs, narratives, folklore, poetry, or heroic tales. Since a warrior code and the life of the warrior is intrinsically and extrinsically connected to the well-being of the human soul, it is not surprising that all codes are connected to cultural religious beliefs and virtues. A warrior code, like a properly executed judo throw, is self-regulating, meaning it is passed down, inherited, maintained, and protected by those who have passed the necessary rites of passage to be considered warriors. They must demonstrate a moral and ethical nobleness of self-sacrifice and willingness to live and die by that code.

---

[29] French, *The Code of the Warrior.*

Warriors and warrior codes model how autonomous agents and heteronomous codes both adhere to rule sets, structures, and social contracts. The model necessitates a healthy tension of rejecting carnal instincts and vices by embracing autonomous moral virtues, while relying upon ethical and behavioral social norms, habits, and attitudes in a mutually dependent relationship for the greater good. For every correct way to execute Osoto Gari, misplaced timing, misunderstanding of an opponent's position, and improper foot and hand placements can lead to being overwhelmed by an opponent. There are sixty-eight Nage-waza (judo throws). Exercising the right one at the right place and time against the right opponent requires habit, instinct, and courage.

We can identify unique similarities and differences in ancient warrior codes such as Greece's Homeric Heroes, Rome's Stoic Legions, the Vikings' Chivalrous Medieval Knights, Indigenous American Tribes, Chinese Shaolin Monks, Japanese Samurai, and Sultan Saladin's Islamic Warriors. Upon further study, we find universal virtues of each code, much like Judo's sixty-eight Naga-waza, and yet engage challenging and sometimes controversial aspects to varying codes which differing cultures may find troublesome. Cardinal virtues such as courage, wisdom, justice, integrity, temperance, faith, hope, love, in conjunction with universal virtues such as honor, respect, courtesy, and sacrifice seem morally sound. However, some virtues unique to specific cultures may be held in question such as ceremonial suicide, revenge, or certain religious practices, depending on the person's cultural lens.

The Greeks believed teaching and training was a two-fold process of imparting wisdom and knowledge into the student and demonstrating understanding through practical application. You can watch YouTube videos of judo throws and teach yourself an academic understanding of the art. However, what you learn when training with an uke (training partner) in a dojo of students is where the habit and instinctual learning takes shape. The wisdom and knowledge gained by cadets at the United States Service Academies—through developing personal codes of virtue, moral and ethical reasoning, and leadership skills—focuses on shaping leaders of character. Today, these qualities are reflected in the life-and-death decisions they make on the battlefields, where they serve as trusted professional warriors.

If true, what kind of psychological moral development do leaders of character experience and ascertain inspiring others to follow them? Coinciding with a theological worldview and historical ethos, psychological moral development reveals further insight regarding how individuals and organizations teach, train, and coach leaders of character.

Justice: Twentieth Century Ethical, Moral, & Social Psychology

The world wars, genocide, and tragic destruction of the human soul during the twentieth century by authoritarian rulers raised up a new type of breed of social, moral, and ethical psychological study. Attempting to understand Nazi Germany's genocidal campaign against the Jews, psychological moral development became of keen interest to men such as Philip Zimbardo, Stanley Milgram, and Lawrence Kohlberg. Studies stretching and sometimes surpassing ethical standards in the field of human obedience, response to external factors, and authority are well known today as controversial and yet, essentially important research proving that "good" people will commit "evil" acts against other "good" people given the right circumstances. Where is the justice? What does it mean for a society, leaders, people in power, or the powerless to understand justice? How do wisdom, courage, and justice work together?

Milgram's 1961 experiment assessing external control factors and people's obedient compliance to authority when asked to electrically shock a victim, really an actor in another room, pushed ethical limits of psychological research. It also proved when people abdicated their moral autonomy and authority to an authority figure who gave them permission to perform a task by rule or command, without any consequence or remorse, the majority of people followed through, regardless of the perceived outcome to the victim. A means of justice was established by an authority and delivered by willing agents, even at times against their own moral conscience and reasoning.

Ten years later, Zimbardo followed suit with the Stanford Prison Experiment, turning young college students into prison guards and prisoners. The two-week experiment lasted less than forty-eight hours due to the horrific abuse the "prison guards" exacted on the "prisoners," proving Zimbardo's theory that if given authority—or if stripped of all authority—social and institutional power dynamics will compel those with authority and power to oppress those without. Once again demonstrating a misuse of justice and the twisted vices of oppression and anarchy.

The experiment stopped when a young PhD psychology assistant's moral compass compelled her to exercise wisdom, courage, and justice demanding he stop the experiment. She had a unique and significant institutional power dynamic over Zimbardo; she was his fiancée and gave him an ultimatum. Fortunately for Zimbardo, and everyone involved in the experiment, he conceded. They are still married today.[30] Her moral reasoning of justice and human flourishing won the day.

Kohlberg's Moral Reasoning

Lawrence Kohlberg is internationally regarded as a pioneer in the study of psychological moral development. Three primary schools of psychological study prevailed in the twentieth century research of how humanity lives moral lives. Freud's prominent psychoanalytic approach focused on how people respond by their feelings, specifically the superego's use of sexual desire and carnal instincts. Hartshorne and May researched the behavior of the human psyche based upon social learning contexts of teaching and training attitudes, habits, and values. However, Kohlberg presents a third contrasting theory, leaning on his extensive study of Immanuel Kant and "conscious moral decision making while

---

[30] Philip Zimbardo, The Lucifer Effect

rejecting cultural and ethical relativism."[31] Kohlberg's personal experiences led him to pursue the universal virtue of justice and study the psychological moral development of morally autonomous agents.

When training jiu-jitsu, there are hundreds of moves a practitioner may choose from, based upon their training and the position they find themselves in with an opponent. Sure, there are dynamic flashy moves, however, many times the basic moves practiced with mastery win. I have watched thousands of wrestling and jiu-jitsu matches where coaches have yelled at the top of their lungs for their athlete to execute a crucial move. Whether the athlete hears them in the heat of battle or not, with time and position usually of the essence, habit and instinct take over and override any other relative view of the match. They act autonomously, of their own accord.

Kohlberg's work has significantly influenced the teaching and training of character-based leadership development for trusted professionals, such as me. I had the privilege of studying under one of Kohlberg's students, Dr. John Snarey, at Emory University. Kohlberg and his students work on moral reasoning, morality, and how moral reasoning changes over the lifetime is paramount in understanding how and why people address interpersonal conflict and how organizations create positive or negative cultures.

In the context of professions, how people are assessed, selected, and trained is paramount to how they operate as morally autonomous agents within a heteronomous ethos. Kohlberg's research begins with the timeless metaphysical question of the nature of virtue, and whether it is acquired intuitively or by repetition, culture, environment, or experience. His essays on moral development and moral reasoning encourage his readers to return to Meno's question to Socrates. "Can you tell me, Socrates, is virtue something that can be taught?"[32] Kohlberg effectively used forty years of

---

[31] Lisa Kuhmerker, Uwe Gielen, and Richard Hayes, *The Kohlberg Legacy for the Helping Professions* (Birmingham: Doxa, 1991), 19.

[32] Kuhmerker, Gielen, and Hayes, *The Kohlberg Legacy for the Helping Professions.*, 21-22.

research and modeling to provide practitioners an effective methodology for teaching moral reasoning.

Kohlberg's quest for universal justice includes the idea that people utilize moral reasoning using norms, modal elements, and value elements to make decisions. Norms provide value to what moral agents deem important such as life, law, and liberty. Modal elements address the mood, expression, or feeling of those norms. Value elements refer to the desired outcomes or consequences of making moral decisions. The three stages of development, pre-conventional, conventional, and post-conventional, each contain two developmental levels for a total of six levels. These stages and levels enable practitioners to categorize autonomous moral agents' development based upon their responses to moral dilemmas and interpersonal conflicts.

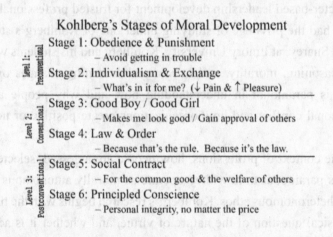

Kohlberg's Stages of Moral Development

Level 1: Preconventional

Stage 1: Obedience & Punishment
– Avoid getting in trouble
Stage 2: Individualism & Exchange
– What's in it for me? (↓ Pain & ↑ Pleasure)

Level 2: Conventional

Stage 3: Good Boy / Good Girl
– Makes me look good / Gain approval of others
Stage 4: Law & Order
– Because that's the rule. Because it's the law.

Level 3: Postconventional

Stage 5: Social Contract
– For the common good & the welfare of others
Stage 6: Principled Conscience
– Personal integrity, no matter the price

Kohlberg's use of moral dilemmas such as the famed Heinz Dilemma assesses moral agents' concepts, norms, elements, and stages of psychological moral development. Furthermore, the stages outline a moral agent's reasoning on what is right, the reasons for doing right, and the social consequences to the moral agent within a heteronomous social contract.[33] Moral agents progress by becoming more matured and refined in exercising their moral autonomy and subsequent moral reasoning within the heteronomous environment by embracing universal virtues such as justice. Level one entails acting within a heteronomous morality of obeying rules, while level six involves the rightful exercise of universal ethical principles as morally autonomous agents who transcend transactional rules for transformational principles at a post-conventional stage. In fact, Kohlberg extends his stage theory by proposing a religious stage seven, something that even exceeds the universal ethical principles of stage six. This acknowledgment "rests on the metaphysical and religious assumptions consistent with, but reducible to, rational science and morality."

From my Christian worldview, this is like the spiritual process of sanctification, experiencing God's vertical attributes of love and justice upon our lives and developing our horizontal praxis within humanity. Understanding Kohlberg's psychological and philosophical theory empowers people of faith to effectively lead as moral agents in the public square. Utilizing Judeo-Christian norms and values, practicing the behavioral habits and attitudes of such an ethos, and acknowledging and subsequently resisting the carnality of the superego, faith-based leaders play a pivotal role as trusted moral agents in the public square in a myriad of professions. From a philosophical virtue-based lens, so goes the process for teaching, training, and empowering leaders of character.

Not surprisingly, Kohlberg's work is not without criticism. His cognitive development approach has faced adversity over forty years of research. Initially, many thought his theory would not transcend cultures, however, his global research from the United States, Japan, India, and Israel proved the validity of his theory. In the late 1970s, he faced criticism that his work was chauvinistic and exclusive to men, however, Kohlberg's

---

[33] Kuhmerker, Gielen, and Hayes, *The Kohlberg Legacy for the Helping Professions.*

research in phenomenological identification and concern for universal justice refutes those allegations as well.[34]

Weathering the storm of critics, Kohlberg's work has global ramifications today. The ethical decision-making model utilized in the US Army's Professional Military Education (PME) was developed by Dr. James Rest, one of Kohlberg's longtime students and personal friends. The model's deontological approach provides an effective framework for trusted moral agents to make ethically based decisions, emphasizing the virtues and values of professionals and their respected professional codes and laws. However, it does not address in depth the psychological moral development of those agents and understanding why, what, and how they think critically. In an oversaturated world of information, leaders of character must learn how to process general information into actionable intelligence, critically, morally, and ethically thinking along the way. Plato encouraged virtuous people and organizations to exercise temperance when using wisdom, courage, and justice collectively to pursue moral excellence.

Liberating the Oppressed and Punishing the Oppressor

In my lifetime, I have experienced being oppressed by opposing positions and toxic leadership, verbally threatened, physically assaulted for standing my ground, and faced unfounded investigations and character assassination because of my moral courage. These experiences shaped me to advocate for those oppressed and punish the oppressor.

On one of my several combat deployments I was startled awake when there was a knock on my "hooch" plywood door in the middle of the night. I opened the door and a young soldier from our brigade stood in the doorway, visibly shaking and nervously explaining to me that if "they" knew he was talking to me, "they" would kill him. I assured him of his

---

[34] Carol Gilligan, "In a Different Voice: Women's Conceptions of Self and of Morality," *Harvard Educational Review* 47, no. 4 (1977): 481–517.

confidentiality with me as a chaplain and he sat down. He proceeded to unpack a situation with a fellow soldier in the organization. One with a very compromised character and poor reputation. The soldier's poor performance and unprofessional conduct had landed her in my office and our psychologist's office on multiple occasions. Her chain of command had built a substantial legal packet on her for each offense, primarily that of offering sexual favors to other soldiers. She lost rank, and as a result she also lost pay, and now had such offenses on her military record. Yet, they kept her in the unit. After all, it was combat, and we needed her particular skills.

My conversations with her were difficult. The wounds she carried from past physical, psychological, and verbal abuse prior to the military came to the forefront under the duress of a combat deployment. She was a wounded soul who lost the ability to flourish spiritually, mentally, and physically. It broke my heart. And whenever we spoke, something just wasn't right. I couldn't put my finger on it, but something was awry. That hunch was confirmed when the soldier who came to me in her defense shared the rest of the story and triggered my deep virtue of justice. The soldier claimed that members of her chain of command (her boss and boss's boss) were using their authority and rank to prosecute her under UCMJ (Uniform Code of Military Justice) as a cover. A cover? For *what*?

The soldier explained that it was a cover for using her personally for sexual favors. They built a substantial counseling and UCMJ file on her to cover their immoral, unethical, and horrendous behavior. I was irate and enraged, and I wanted justice. But how? How should I approach this with wisdom? Who should I speak with without violating confidentiality and compromising the soldier in question, or the one who had the courage to report it. What would be this group of leaders' response? Would they physically attack her, the soldier in question as he posed, or even me, the chaplain? What should I do? How should I exercise all three virtues with temperance? I ensured the soldier his information was safe with me and got his permission to pursue this at a higher level without involving him.

I prayed about it and exercised my ethical decision-making process. I decided to bring it to the senior non-commissioned officer (NCO) who would have direct influence over the situation. We had a healthy relationship and worked well together.

When I posed the situation, he told me to stay out of it because it was "not in my lane." He questioned my sources and the story as a whole, but I pushed back. NCOs, let alone senior NCOs, like Command Sergeant Majors (CSM), aren't used to getting a lot of push back, especially from a chaplain. I needed a trigger to compel him to act.

What I did know was that he was affiliated with an external social-civic organization, along with these leaders in question, which has its own chain of command and loyalty. I was brief. I told him he had twenty-four hours to decide whether he would perform his duties loyally as a senior non-commissioned officer or choose the loyalty of the external organization. Predictably, he got upset, shared some choice words with me, and told me to get out of his office. The next day, he took the appropriate action. The soldier was removed from the toxic environment of that unit and provided the help and resources she needed. The chain of command involved in the immoral and unethical behavior were placed under investigation and eventually prosecuted.

Because of this experience, I now serve as a board member and chaplain for an organization called Skull Games, led by one of my great friends who I had a privilege to serve with in the Army, Lieut. Gen. (Ret.) Jeff Tiegs. Skull Games hunts predators, sex traffickers, and anyone involved in the human trafficking industry that buys and sells children, women, and men for sex. Skull Games members are morally and ethically convicted leaders of character grounded in wisdom, courage, justice, and temperance, who with their unique skills, hunt predators and support law enforcement agencies to end human trafficking.

Kohlberg's model accurately depicts my psychological moral development and those of leaders who I've served with. Learning to practice wisdom, courage, justice, and temperance in adverse environments has manifested transformational growth in my leadership, pursuing human flourishing for myself and others. In my military career, I was privileged to work with units whose mottos proclaimed to "free the oppressed" and "oppressors beware."

Knowing who we are as leaders of character significantly shapes how we think morally and ethically in the public square. With such courage, wisdom, justice, temperance, and love, we can restore civility in the public square. Leaders of character transform and impact spheres of influence as thought leaders when their intellectual capacity, guided by a moral and ethical decision-making process, shapes how they and others lead people and teams. Just like the Gracie boys on the beach, we may not always have the luxury of being in a standard ring or octagon. We may find ourselves in a VUCA environment with unstable footing, questionable boundaries, and challenging opponents. We must be aware of our spacing, play our game, and trust our training that has trained our trust to act with the right intent, decision-making process, and courageous leadership.

··· Chapter Seven: Epistemology &
Emotivism in the Public
Square

We have firmly established that who we are, based upon what we believe, provides us with a foundation to think critically and lead effectively in our areas of influence and expertise. If true, then how does a foundation of moral reasoning and ethical decision-making enable us to think epistemologically and lead influentially in any environment that we may find ourselves in? Every human being operates out of some form of moral reasoning. Our morals, what we personally believe is right or wrong, typically stem from religious, philosophical, cultural, educational, and experiential influences in our lives.

Moral philosophy shapes how we see the world, and how we operate in it with our intentions, thoughts, and actions. These include virtue ethics (Aristotle), non-cognitivism (Hume), deontological ethics (Kant), utilitarian ethics (Bentham and Mills), divine command theory

(Augustine), natural law (Aquinas), and cultural relativism / postmodernism (Nietzsche).[35] Each moral philosophy influences and shapes a professional ethos differently. However, I would contest that Nietzsche's philosophy in the context of creating morally autonomous and ethically loyal trusted professionals, lacks systematic or foundational virtues to shape a common ethos due to his stance of rejecting metaphysical and empirical virtues and objective truth. His approach to using subjective morals as a will to power for personal survival does not work well with developing trusted professions and professionals. That mindset typically creates hostile, toxic, and unproductive cultures of questionable leaders of character who violate transformational leadership principles promoting human flourishing and excellence for personal gain and survival.

Moral reasoning, which dictates our moral autonomy, asks the question, "Do I manage problematic tension, or do I immediately solve the problem?" Hence the moral dilemma. I've heard internationally acclaimed author, leader, and pastor Andy Stanley ask this question for years in his teachings and writing. It seems to be an excellent first step in a moral and ethical decision-making model, which is why we use it in ours. When used effectively, moral reasoning pursues a mutually dependent relationship with an ethical norm and ethos.

Ethical decision-making is based upon a professional ethos, rule of law, codes, or creeds. The ethical decision-making process considers what moral virtues must be considered in this decision-making process. How do individual moral virtues align with a professional ethos, or ethic, rules of law, compliance, and standards? Moral and ethical leaders must determine the consequences of their intentions, thought process, and potential actions, and more importantly, whether they are willing to accept responsibility, be held accountable, and take ownership of their decision.

---

[35] Barry Loewer, ed., *30-Second Philosophies: The 50 Most Thought Provoking Philosophies, Each Explained in Half a Minute* (New York: Metro Books, 2010), table of contents.

When trusted leaders of character use an epistemological approach to their moral and ethical decision-making process, they utilize critical thinking, logic, reason, and emotional regulation to make the best decisions possible. This is the third step of the decision-making process, creatively and objectively coming up with multiple courses of action. In the military, we have a process for this called Mission Development and Mission Planning, or MDMP. We use seven steps in our Mission Analysis process to ensure we collectively consider all perspectives, maximize resources, and empower people available to achieve mission success.

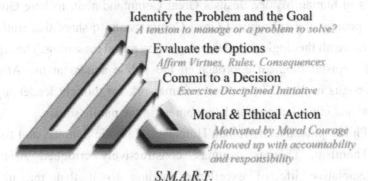

Coaching Moral & Ethical Decision Makers to Make the Right Decisions!
Using the "James Rest Ethical Decision Making Model

Identify the Problem and the Goal
A tension to manage or a problem to solve?

Evaluate the Options
Affirm Virtues, Rules, Consequences

Commit to a Decision
Exercise Disciplined Initiative

Moral & Ethical Action
*Motivated by Moral Courage
followed up with accountability
and responsibility*

S.M.A.R.T.
specific, measurable, achievable, relevant, time oriented

The final step to the essence of who we are, how we think, and how we lead is when we exercise moral courage to carry out our course of action with passion, purpose, and precision. A trusted leader of character's decision-making process does not begin with four logical steps of reason. Rather, it effectively operates from a greater depth of understanding who they are as a leader of character and how they interact with the world around them. For me, I find that epistemological depth in theology, philosophy, and history as these disciplines address the human soul's need to flourish in a compromised and imperfect world. Leaders of character who create psychologically affirming spaces of curious, creative, and constructive epistemological thinking must restore a public square of human flourishing from the current polarities of secularist exclusion and religious totalitarianism.

Theologically, Dr. Miroslav Volf, the Henry B. Wright Professor of Theology and director of the Yale Center for Faith and Culture at Yale University, writes that the Judeo-Christian prophetic voice of experiential ascent and descent fostering a relationship with a transformational God offers humanity the greatest hope in contemplating true happiness and living a virtuous life.[36] The Ten Commandments, one of the first ethical codes in human history, Jesus's Great Commandment, to love God and love people, and subsequent Great Commission, to share that truth with others are all theological statements guiding moral reasoning. The Apostle Paul's epistemological approach in the public square at the Athenian Areopagus in Acts 17 provides a framework for thought leadership and moral and ethical character development in the public square.

Philosophically, the Italian Humanist, Catholic Scholar, and founder of Thomism, Thomas Aquinas, constructively critiqued Aristotle's contemplative life of excellence, adding to it that the ultimate advancement in pursuing truth and happiness is in the contemplation of God. Aquinas's resuscitation of Greek philosophy and human flourishing renewed the pursuit of human liberty and freedom within the rule of law and just war from the thirteenth century to more modern documents of western democracy such as the Mayflower Compact, Declaration of Independence, Constitution of the United States, and Bill of Rights.

Public institutions on display and scrutinized in the public square, such as the United States Army (that currently operates in over one hundred and sixty countries), have a moral and ethical responsibility for maximizing

---

[36] Volf, *A Public Faith*, 6-8.

human flourishing through teaching and training a moral and ethical professional ethos, thereby producing greater soldiers of character. The timeless theological and philosophical virtues found in the documents listed above establish the bedrock of the United States Army's Professional Ethic, which is founded upon a sense of duty to live a flourishing life and defend the rights of others to do the same by swearing an oath to defend the US Constitution.

Theological and Philosophical Foundation

Scripture establishes the theological framework of human flourishing. Aristotle was likely familiar with Jewish law. Aquinas studied the Old and New Testaments, Augustine, and the early church fathers' writings. Human flourishing may be summarized by the Westminster Catechism's first question: "What is the chief end of man? Man's chief end is to glorify God and to enjoy him forever."[37] Romans 11:36 states, "For from him and through him and to him are all things. To him be glory forever." 1 Corinthians 10:31 instructs Christians, "So, whether you eat or drink, or whatever you do, do all to the glory of God." A theological pursuit of human flourishing must include a spiritually virtuous intent to pursue by faith and with critical reasoning the wisdom, knowledge, and understanding of the truth and love of God. Whether autonomously or in a heteronomous social contract, humanity upholds human flourishing when a theological a priori foundation and a right intent shapes moral and ethical action, which should lead to the telos to glorify God and enjoy his eternal goodness.

Human flourishing preserves the Imago Dei. Unfortunately, due to the depravity of the human soul, the very institution and people who should practice this way of life of excellence has, despite best efforts and intent,

---

[37] Westminster Assembly, *The Shorter Catechism with Scripture Proofs* (New Zealand: Titus Books, 2014), 1.

fallen short many times as well. The civil public square would do well to remember Micah 6:8 to "act justly, love mercy, and walk humbly."

The American social contract sprung from a corresponding spirit within the virtuous character of the Founding Fathers and their theological foundation in the Old and New Testaments. President John Adams declared the eighteenth-century philosophies regarding the "perfectibility of man" to be "abstracted from all divine authority" and completely unacceptable.[38] He writes, "It is an idea of the Christian religion, and ever has been of all believers of the immortality of the soul, that the intellectual part of man is capable of progressive improvement forever. Where then is the sense of calling the perfectibility of man an original idea or modern discovery ... I consider the perfectibility of man as used by modern philosophers to be mere words without a meaning, that is mere nonsense."[39] The intellectual part of people cannot improve humanity without acknowledging the immortality of the soul.

The American experiment of a representative democracy was developed and has roots in Cromwell's England, the Magna Carta, Rome's republic, and the Greek's Athenian democratic city state. However, according to scholars such as Os Guinness and Rabbi Jonathan Sacks, our nation's moral and ethical foundation is rooted primarily in the Jewish Exodus story and the covenantal Ten Commandments found in Exodus 20.

Guinness writes, "The heart of the Exodus story is a template for society, for human personhood, for freedom, for justice, and for social change that shaped the American Revolution in highly practical ways. So much so that it has been truly said that Exodus and its influence on freedom long preceded Athens."[40] Dr. Martin Luther King Jr.'s use of the Exodus story in many of his speeches established a theological foundation for the civil rights movement pursuit of human flourishing. Undoubtedly, the character and virtue of our American liberty and freedoms have a theological foundation.

---

[38] David McCullough, *John Adams* (New York: Simon & Schuster, 2001), 591.
[39] Ibid.
[40] Guiness, *The Last Call for Liberty*, 23.

America's Founding Fathers' deliberation over the Declaration of Independence, rejection of the Articles of Confederation, and principled acceptance of the United States Constitution, including the successive Bill of Rights and its' amendments, are a modern example of pursuing the theory of human flourishing by working to secure the rights of life, liberty, and the pursuit of happiness. The Ten Commandments and the covenant made by all of Israel before God set a framework for such a Constitutional covenant that includes a "freely chosen consent, morally binding pledge, and reciprocal responsibility of all for all."[41]

As an example, it is to this Constitution, a rule of law, that every US military service member takes an oath, making a modern-day covenant with themselves and their nation, to uphold its moral and ethical virtues. The Constitution is not a perfect document, and the oath of office is not a promise of perfectly defending it. It is an oath to faithful practice to defend an ideal striving for the pursuit of human flourishing and a more perfect union. Such an oath compels individuals of moral and ethical conviction and character to defend it with their lives out of a sense of duty, *Pro Deo Et Patria* (for God and country). This oath of office and duty to a rule of law is contrary to a contractual compliance of autocratic rulers, or rule of man.

So, returning to our warrior ethos example of professional and professions, teaching, and training morally and ethically sound warriors require more than just an oath of office. It requires a mindset and practice of lifelong learning and soulful contemplation of pursuing the truth of what human flourishing entails as a warrior class. It requires the heart and soul of the warrior to flourish first and foremost before cognitive agility or physical dominance. High character, high culture organizations align to a similar process of creating professionals and a professional ethos.

Jesus's account of the sower, the seed, and the soil in Matthew 13 illustrates this reality. This parable teaches that the sower (Jesus Christ) and the seed (God's word) are unchanging, tested, and true. The sower

---

[41] Os Guiness., 26-29.

unconditionally spreads seed across four different types of soil, however, only one bears fruit. The only subjective condition determining the success of the sower's efforts and the seed's potential is the quality of the soil in which it germinates. "But he who received seed on the good ground is he who hears the word and understands it, who indeed bears fruit and produces: some a hundredfold, some sixty, some thirty" (Matthew 13:23). The seed of human flourishing is sown in the soul.

Jesus's Great Commandment (Matthew 22:36-40) and Great Commission (Matthew 28) require the character of one's heart to embrace human flourishing and happiness through practicing the truth and love of Jesus Christ and sharing it with the world. The commandment calls believers to love God first and love others second. The commission calls us to share that love with humanity to the ends of the earth. The secular worldview rejects these commands and commissions outright, instead advocating that people love themselves first, hence removing the need or existence of a God, and the need or existence of a Christian faith with a metaphysical ascent and descent of contemplating the truth of God.

Today's secular worldview rejects the concept of practicing a contemplative love of God and instead values what Alasdair McIntyre calls emotivism, which is culturally defined happiness consisting of instant gratification, self-absorption, and individual pampering.[42] Miroslav Volf writes, "It is important to keep focused on God and on the proper understanding of human flourishing. For this, in the end, is what the Christian faith as a prophetic religion is all about—being an instrument of God for the sake of human flourishing, in this life and the next."[43] When Christians—as instruments of God—teach, train, and apply God's word in the public square, we effectively share the gospel to all who hear so that they may flourish in this life and the next by experiencing joy with the Creator rather than the temporal vice of the world's narcissistic happiness.

---

[42] Alasdair MacIntyre, *After Virtue* (Notre Dame: University of Notre Dame Press, 1984).
[43] Volf, *A Public Faith*, 5.

The Apostle Paul's polemical approach to being all things to all people in Acts 17 exhibits a model example of how Christians can effectively teach, train, and live out the gospel in the public square. Paul's use of Greek philosophy, Roman culture, and Jewish law is wrongly depicted by fundamentalist Christians as syncretistic. Paul's sound creation theology and use of general revelation, in conjunction with the special revelation of Christ, establishes a steadfast and firm foundation of the gospel in the public square.

Paul proclaims everything is taken captive by Christ because everything was created by and through Christ (1 Cor 3:18-25, 2 Cor 10:5, Col 1:17). Paul's concept of human flourishing is rooted firmly in his theological conviction of Christ's resurrection. This enabled him to be all things to all people, meeting those in the public square where they themselves were rooted, which was in the philosophy and religion of the day. Today, Christians can follow this same wisdom to meet others where they are to facilitate epistemological dialogue, expression, and mutual respect in the public square. The public square is a space for everyone to respectfully be heard and seen, and for everyone who wants to be heard and seen respect and uphold the civic principles of a public square.

Paul challenged the major pagan worship and philosophies of his day in conjunction with teaching about how Christ's life, death, and resurrection fulfilled the Jewish prophecies. In Acts 17, Luke recounts Paul's masterful approach. Paul begins in the synagogue, which should have been a place of cultural comfort, even though he was carrying a dangerous message. Then Paul moves into the syncretistic marketplace to deliver a clarifying message to the people. Finally, Paul teaches in Athens' exclusively dangerous forum, the Areopagus, or Mars Hill, proclaiming his message of hope in something greater than us, referring to the Greek's "unknown god." At the end of the day, some followed Paul, some asked him to return to answer more questions, and some mocked him. Nothing has changed in two thousand years.

N.T. Wright springboards off Cicero's classification of first century philosophical classifications to illustrate Paul's polemical method.[44] Cicero classified the philosophies into three categories: Academic, Stoic, and Epicurean. Paul skillfully addressed Cicero's skeptical Academic, disciplined Stoic, and emotive Epicurean's intellectual part of man with the immortality of the soul. Paul compared these finite philosophies and mythical gods with the infinite "one true God, the God of Abraham, Isaac, and Jacob," who was revealed through the resurrection of Jesus Christ and by subsequent personal and collective encounters with over five hundred people, including Paul.

Postmodern and progressive academicians have long strayed from practicing classical liberal education in the halls of premier institutions founded upon theological tradition. Instead, skepticism and moral relativism from the schools of Nietzsche, Foucault, and Gramsci transformed institutions of academic rigor and the study of human flourishing through theology, moral virtues, and classical ethics to centers of modern-day Orwellian group—think intellectual and spiritual debauchery. These movements, aimed to create space by removing God, instead created a void and showed the need for God. This space drew in the fledgling soul that craved a return of theological and classical virtue ethics, moral and ethical decision-making, and principles of leading a life promoting human flourishing, back to the public square in search of truth in God.

To the Stoic, Paul affirmed the logical order and nature of the universe through God's general revelation. He stretched their philosophy beyond the recognition that the world is somehow divine to the truth about the world in its present and future states. He taught that both the world and heaven will be made new. This eternal resurrected life, absent in Stoic philosophy, is entirely the creation of the one and only, Logos, divine God.

Finally, Paul countered the Epicureans' belief that God was distant from, or unconcerned with, the world. Instead, he encouraged Epicureans

---

[44] N. T. Wright, *What St. Paul Really Said*, Grand Rapids, Michigan: Wm. B. Eerdmans, 1997

to consider a greater pursuit than simply finding pleasure, love, and emotional fulfillment in the temporal world. By trusting and believing that Jesus Christ passionately and compassionately involved himself in the world for his glory and for our salvation, we can find both temporal and eternal joy in him. God did this through the general revelation of his creation, and by, with, and through the special revelation and unconditional love of Christ's death and resurrection.

Over two thousand years later, Paul's message promoting that true human flourishing is found in the omniscient, omnipresent, logical, compassionate, personal, true divine God, Jesus Christ, still produces the same results that it did at the Areopagus. Like those in Paul's day, some people believe, some ask questions and seek information, and others reject the notion entirely. This is a healthy public square that creates space for those who believe, desire greater contemplation, or resolutely dissent. Today, I believe, faith in the public square continues to be spiritually compelling, intellectually validating, and an existential praxis of the gospel.

Bridging the Gap from a First Century to a Twenty-First Century Public Square

Cicero's philosophical classifications remain helpful. Like Paul, Christians today must address the skeptics who question objective truth, virtue ethics, and character development. We must validate the logic, reasoning, and purposeful and disciplined way of life for the Stoic through character development. We cannot fail to empathetically connect with the souls of Epicureans and their need for relationship and connection during character development. The answers to their questions can be found in the grace and love of the gospel. In the modern public square, the necessity of the gospel conversation and human flourishing, like Paul at the Areopagus, may be bridged with engaging theology, philosophy, science, history, and ethics, i.e., epistemological thinking. Finding space in a public square hostile to religion and metaphysics may seem to be an obstacle, however, as Stoic philosophy highlights, *the obstacle is the way.*

The Enlightenment Project, named by philosopher Alisdair MacIntyre, attempted to annihilate the legitimacy of objective truth, religion, and virtue ethics and replace them with forms of modern humanism and utilitarianism. God was replaced, as was a deontological concept of right intent, reasoning, and action, with Hume's non-cognitive, emotive relativism. MacIntyre defines emotivism as "the doctrine that all evaluative judgments and more specifically all moral judgments are nothing but expressions of preference, expressions of attitude, or feeling."[45] In hindsight, movements shaped by Nietzsche's ideas of the "will to power" and the Ubermensch, from the modern to postmodern era, exacerbated the depravity of humanity, twisted the definition of human flourishing, and fragmented the identity of the soul. The social experiment to define human flourishing without God failed miserably as demonstrated by the twentieth century's socialist and communist movements.

The undertow of secular humanism and postmodern thought puts at risk an individual or society's ability to flourish. It promulgates fragmented personalities, exacerbated by social media platforms and confused identities founded upon syncretistic and conflicting worldviews. Terry Eagleton writes, "In post-Nietzschean spirit, the West appears to be busily undermining its own erstwhile metaphysical foundations with an unholy mélange of practical materialism, political pragmatism, moral and cultural relativism, and philosophical skepticism."[46] Humans now separate their personalities, compartmentalize their beliefs, and think, feel, and act differently personally and professionally, rejecting a unified ethos in pursuit of excellence, or as Aristotle said, eudemonia.[47] Fragmented identities and worldviews create morally lost people in ambiguous and

---

[45] MacIntyre, *After Virtue*, 12.

[46] Terry Eagleton, "Culture and Barbarism: Metaphysics in a Time of Terrorism," *Commonwealth*, March 27, 2009, https://www.commonwealmagazine.org/culture-barbarism-0.

[47] Paul Berghaus and Nathan Cartegena, "Developing Good Soldiers: The Problem of Fragmentation in the Army," *Journal of Military Ethics* 12, no. 4 (January 20, 2014): 287–303.

complex environments, lacking the a priori principles, moral reasoning, and empathy to adhere to a common ethos.

Vulnerable, cognitively dissonant, psychologically fragmented, and subjectively grounded, our society is ripe for exploitation of Orwellian thought control. With the rapid advancement of AI technology, unhindered by strong ethics and compliance, some forms, uses, and abuses of AI threaten human flourishing, compromising how we think, what we think, and how we act in the public square. AI is not the problem. It's been around longer than we think, if we consider the use of the computer and machines through the twentieth century. It is a rapidly expanding tool. The problem is how it can be manipulated and used for power and control over the human soul, and society as a whole.

Answering the question of the purpose of humanity through Aquinas's theological lens and Aristotle's philosophical lens addresses these obstacles and a more excellent way. Pursuing a life of human flourishing requires pursuing the Creator's objective truth and finding joy in pursuing such excellence. To find the means of excellence, one must also be aware of the vices of excess and deficiency. One must be able to draw and find the center of the circles using some sort of a priori principles, rules, laws, and tools. This includes improving rules of law and the ethical use of AI.

For the military, professionals must teach, train, and internalize the principles and virtues of a professional ethic to protect it and those they have vowed by oath of office to protect.[48] For leaders in other professions, they have a similar code or creed. For the citizen, we must reflect on Plato's Meno and the second half of the quote we have yet to reveal. "Can you tell me, Socrates, is virtue something that can be taught? Or does it come by practice? Or is it neither teaching nor practice but natural aptitude or instinct?" What if it is collectively a blend of aptitude, instinct, teaching, and practice? That seems to be a more holistic approach to human flourishing.

---

[48] Some material in this project comes from previous work: Anthony Randall, "ET703 Church and Religion in the Public Square" (August 21, 2019), 703.

The aptitude to pursue epistemological thinking rooted in virtue and character development provides the necessary foundation for leaders to promote human flourishing out of who they are and how they think. In an overly informed world bombarded by syncretistic concepts, epistemological study develops keen instinctual awareness to discerning what is true and the courage, confidence, and courtesy to create space for dialogue. Teaching and training bring clarity to over stimulated senses and emotions. They expand myopic worldviews confined by dogma and lacking the art of critical thinking. Teaching and training challenges what a truly inclusive public square looks and sounds like to promote human flourishing. Finally, epistemological thinking empowers Aristotle's pursuit of practicing a life of excellence and the Apostle Paul's pursuit of a more excellent way through loving God and people.

Transformational thought leaders transform the public square by knowing who they are, how they think, and how they lead, appealing to the Academic's pursuit of wisdom, the Epicureans love for life, and the Stoics disciplined practice of a life well lived. Moving from philosophy to action requires aligning our passion (calling), purpose (gifts and abilities), and precision (our public square) in how we practice a life of excellence. Transformational leaders are more than influencers seeking dopamine hits from sales, likes, followers, and subscribers. Transformational moral leaders are thought leaders who lead with influence to transform the public square for all to flourish. Each of us leads differently, and each of us can lead with influence. How we lead, based upon who we are and how we think using emotional intelligence, is the next step in our journey to practicing excellence.

··· Chapter Eight: The OG, " W,"

& EQ Leadership

The artist formerly known as Prince changed his name to a symbol. Twitter is now X. Social influencers identify themselves with letters, numbers, or just an image. The forty-third President of the United States was known in pop political culture as "W." Before all the OGs and "W"s in our world today, there was a man of character, a moral and ethical decision-maker, and an emotionally intelligent leader (before EI/EQ was even a thing). I like to refer to him as the "OG W." President George Washington. Join me for a moment, eyes closed. (Well, open them to read the book. But … you know what I mean, right?)

It's Christmas night, December 25, 1776. You and I are huddled around a small fire that is heating the same kettle of stone soup we have been eating for the last five days with our fellow colonials in the rag tag Continental Army. Cold, disillusioned, exhausted, sick, and wet, we are seriously questioning the "cause" that we signed up for six months earlier, when the Continental Congress declared independence from the British throne. Things have not worked out as planned. You are missing a boot and fighting off frostbite on your foot, which is wrapped in an array of loose cloth. The thin overcoat, that I wear to work in my fields, cannot keep me warm against the chilling wind coming off the western banks of the Delaware River, across our encampment in eastern Pennsylvania. Nothing's changed over two hundred and forty-eight years. Congress still cannot pass a budget, and we haven't been paid in three months. As we reflect on our family traditions back home—church services, ample food, delightful sweets, songs, and presents under the tree—we stare out into the dark grey wood line, feeling hopeless knowing there is a far superior enemy out there lurking to kill us.

Then he approaches. Freshly powdered wig, wearing his best Christmas day generalissimo uniform, the "OG W."

"Merry Christmas, patriots."

We look away, pretending that if we don't see him, he's not there. General Washington expresses his empathy for our current state, enduring it with us. He acknowledges the truth of the current state of affairs, politically and militarily. He implores us to remain true to the cause of freedom, liberty, and justice for all, even though some of our enlistment contracts are expiring or expired. He encourages us to press on just one more day.

The "OG W" has a mission for us. He explains that he and one of his colonels, an old fisherman from Maine, have found and acquired some boats down by the river. They might not all even float! Here's the mission. In the dark of night and early hours of 26 December, we are going to load up onto those boats, break ice across the Delaware River, land several miles upstream from our target, march several miles in the snow, and at the crack of dawn attack a fortified compound of crack Hessian mercenaries—who outnumber us three to one—in Trenton, NJ. It sounds crazy … but just crazy enough to motivate us to do it.

The rest is history. Speed, surprise, and violence of action led to victory that day for the Continental Army. To this day (apologies to our great citizens of New Jersey), I've never seen anyone work harder to get to Trenton than that rag tag band of patriots. Did the Battle of Trenton strategically turn the military tide of the Revolutionary War as much as other battles that kept the British from cutting off the New England colonies from the mid-Atlantic and southern colonies? Probably not. But what General Washington *did* win was the soul of his army to continue fighting another day, and the hope of a young nation on the brink of losing their short-lived freedom from tyranny. Historically, Washington is not known for his acumen when it comes to military operations as a commander. However, his character, critical thinking, and emotional intelligence won more than a battle and a war. It won the trust, loyalty, and faithfulness of his fellow citizens and nation.

Many definitions of leadership exist, to include defining different types of leadership. The Army's definition of leadership has not changed over the thirty years since I began my military journey. FM 6-22 states that leadership is "the process of influencing people by providing purpose, direction, and motivation while operating to accomplish the mission and improve the organization."[49] In short, *Leadership is influence.* Understanding self, others, organizations, and how to manage them all successfully demonstrates certain attributes defined as emotional intelligence (EQ/EI). EQ's competencies, attributes, and six leadership styles are learned, trained, and implemented by high functioning leaders. Yes, that's the good news. Unlike our IQ, which we seem to be relatively stuck with, anyone can learn and grow their EQ.

Emotionally Intelligent Leadership

Daniel Goleman, Richard Boyatzis, and Annie McKee's work on emotional intelligence over the last three decades is the gold standard for any trusted professional. The complexity of the public square requires leaders to understand and apply emotional intelligence (EQ), which is the

---

[49] FM 6-22, Headquarters, Department of the Army, June 2015

study of neuroscience, behavioral and cognitive psychology, and high performing leadership principles and methodologies. Their book, *Primal Leadership*, explains the theory of EQ founded on neuroscience researching self-awareness and social awareness. EQ includes the ability to lead with certain competencies and attributes. Additionally, EQs four competencies and twelve attributes are found in six EQ leadership styles.[50]

The four EQ domains include self-awareness, self-management, social awareness, and relationship management. Within these domains exist twelve attributes: emotional self-awareness, emotional self-control, adaptability, achievement orientation, positive outlook, empathy, organizational awareness, influence, inspirational leadership, coach and mentor, conflict management, and teamwork. When learned, practiced, and effectively applied, these attributes are regularly reflected within resonant and dissonant leadership styles. Resonant leadership styles effectively build capacity and potential most of the time. Dissonant leadership styles may effectively build capacity and potential sometimes, however, if used too often they result in toxic and unproductive leadership. High EQ leaders can learn, practice, and apply all six leadership styles with the right people at the right time in the right scenario. There are four resonant leadership styles, that when implemented on a regular basis build high character and high culture teams.

Visionary leadership involves moving people to a common goal especially in times of change or new direction. In 2002, I had the opportunity to interview Mr. Jim Kimsey for my first book, *The Vanguard Factor*. When I asked him where he would like to meet, he told me come by his office. He said it was easy to find: Penthouse, Mills Building, 1700 Pennsylvania Avenue. You know, the building next to the other building on Pennsylvania Avenue, where the President of the United States lives. He welcomed me into his office, which included two walls that were glass from the floor to ceiling. He asked me to stand at the apex of the windows, look out, and tell me what I could see. I saw all of Washington DC in

---

[50] Goleman, Daniel, Primal Leadership, Harvard Business Review, 2004.

panoramic form. It was majestic. He asked me if I knew who Pericles was, the great soldier statesmen and ruler of Athens. I assured him that I did. He told me that he was the modern-day Pericles of Washington DC. His vision was to make DC rich with culture, a beacon of education, government, and cornerstone of economic growth. That's the voice of a visionary leader. So, how did he get there?

Dismissed and bounced around high schools due to behavior, he briefly attended Georgetown University and left for financial reasons. Kimsey then attended and graduated from West Point in 1962. Following three tours in Vietnam and the Dominican Republic as an Airborne Ranger, he went on to successfully opening multiple bars around DC in the 1970s. In the 1980s, he joined Quantum Computer Services and became the co-founder and CEO of what we know today as America Online (AOL). He went on to become a billionaire and used it for good. He started the Kimsey Foundation, was Chairman Emeritus of Refugees International, and donated millions of dollars rebuilding Washington DC's arts, education, and sports. He funded West Point's state of the art Division I Athletic Kimsey Center Complex. He provided scholarships for all three service academy students to participate in key branches of government. During the interview, Kimsey told me something I will never forget.

"It is difficult for others to believe in you if you don't believe in yourself. The reason the quiet guy usually stands out is self-confidence. If you can demonstrate that in a calm way and make others feel comfortable, then they will follow you. People gain influence by the trust of other people."[51] Visionary leaders inspire people to accomplish seemingly unachievable things. Visionaries believe in their passion, purpose, and precision by practicing excellence at every step. They share their view of what they see, expect, and know it can be accomplished. In a world where the bell curve of mediocrity tells people to under promise and over deliver, visionary leaders over promise and over deliver.

---

[51] Randall, Anthony, The Vanguard Factor, Integrity House Publishing, 2002. 176.

Coaching leadership is the ability to connect people to a common goal, moving from an individual to a collective identity. I've had the opportunity to work with some of greatest athletic coaches in professional and college sports. The Pittsburgh Pirates were arguably one of the worst teams in Major League Baseball with twenty consecutive losing seasons from 1992 to 2012. A small market team running on less than $100 million a year playing against teams with billion-dollar payrolls.

Clint Hurdle, one of the "winningest" managers in Major League Baseball, his coaching staff, front office, and executive team turned that around becoming one of the "winningest" teams in MLB from 2013-2018, playing in three consecutive postseasons. With General Manager Neal Huntington and Assistant General Manager Kyle Stark, Clint and his staff rebuilt an organization around high character players with winning attributes. They had three goals focused on character, culture, and championship mindset. Build boys to men. Reconnect a city to a team. Win a world championship. I was privilege to spend eight seasons with the organization as a chaplain and leadership coach from 2013-2020 as we accomplished the first two goals. While the third goal eluded us, that coaching leadership style permeates organizations across the MLB, college, and high school programs today in the coaches and players it produced.

I'm 5'6", so when I showed up to work beside those who went on to become the 2016-2017 NCAA Division I Runner Up Gonzaga Men's Basketball Team and 2018-2019 Big 12 Championship Baylor Men's Basketball Team, it was glaringly obvious ... I wasn't there to work on jump shots, layups, man-to-man defense, or 1-3-1 offense. While I was privileged to conduct weekend leadership development retreats for the players and staff, I was honored and humbled to watch Hall of Fame bound coaches like Mark Few and Scott Drew build championship staffs and teams compelling high performing individuals to play as one with passion, purpose, and precision. Today, as an International Coaching Federation credentialed coaching school, we emphasize leadership coaching as a highly effective leadership style to build character and develop winning cultures of excellence. These coaches emulated the art of creating a space to train, asking powerful questions, actively listening, evoking awareness in their players, facilitating their growth, empowering their staff and players, and drawing out their fullest potential.

Affiliative leadership creates harmony and human connection via empathy. Empathy is not an on or off switch. It's not an attribute a leader does or does not possess. Empathy is like a dimmer switch in your living room. We all have empathy. The question is how do we use it effectively? EQ leaders use empathy best when they regulate how brightly, or dimly, they need to use it to set the conditions of a room. The 2000 election created one of the most divisive periods of time in our nation's history. The "hanging chad" controversy and subsequent election results were upsetting. On 9/11, that all changed when our nation was attacked by terrorists set upon destroying our nation's principles of liberty, justice, freedom, and way of life.

By late afternoon, our nation and the world was in a state of shock and grief. President George W. Bush visited Ground Zero in New York City. Standing atop a pile of World Trade Center rubble, the President of the United States revealed his ability to exercise affiliative leadership in the most divisive, destructive, and distressed environment possible. While addressing the crowd of first responders, several told him, "We can't hear you." His response was natural. No script. No teleprompters. No notecards. Just affiliative leadership.

"I can hear you. The rest of the world hears you. And the people who knocked down these buildings will hear all of us soon."[52]

An apolitical statement that united a nation in a moment of grief. Affiliative leadership exercises the dimmer switch of empathy with passion, purpose, and precision. When practiced well, it builds winning

---

[52] https://www.georgewbushlibrary.gov/explore/exhibits/911-steel-american-resolve#:~:text=In%20the%20days%20following%20September,and%20comforted%20a%20grievi ng%20nation.

cultures, positive climates, and holds teams together in the face of adversity.

Finally, democratic leadership embraces collective input by honoring individual perspectives and enhancing collective buy-in to accomplish goals. Young second lieutenants learn very quickly they may outrank everyone in the platoon, but they don't have the collective experience of a team of seasoned non-commissioned officers (NCOs). For those who quickly learn to work collectively with their NCOs, they typically experience successful leadership time as a platoon leader and career progression. For those who aren't quick to embrace democratic leadership, preferring autocratic, hierarchical, and commanding leadership, typically find themselves quickly replaced. Democratic leadership ensures everyone in the management team, executive leadership team, c-suite has a seat and a voice at the table. Democratic leadership emphasizes the power of many unified as one.

Exercising democratic leadership demonstrates a leader's understanding that people are "worthwhile." That word is two words combined into one. "Worth" is the function of value, and "while" is the function of time. When leaders exercise democratic leadership and create a culture passionate about teamwork, purposeful about giving everyone a voice, and precise about moving forward as a team, people feel worthwhile. Their value of who they are, how they think, and how they lead as a teammate along with their time and energy is appreciated, valued, and rewarded.

Resonant leadership styles should be employed on a regular basis. We each have a default resonant leadership style that aligns with our psychological makeup, personality, and leadership philosophy. High EQ leaders learn how to practice all four effectively at the right time and place, with the right group of people to pursue excellence. However, there are situations where dissonant leadership styles may be beneficial instead. One of the two dissonant styles of leadership is pacesetting leadership, which is a high risk and high reward fast-paced style. When used with high performing and competent teams, it is very successful, however, if used too long or with a poorly performing group, it fails. During my time serving in special operations, I was surrounded by pacesetting leadership. Pacesetting leaders bring their "A" game every day, and when everyone else does as well, winning is the standard. Aligned passion, purpose, and precision pursuing excellence is the norm. It is an exciting environment, running hard with high character, high performance teammates.

However, we may not always be on an "A" team with "A" team leaders and players. When pacesetting leadership is used in different environments to break paradigms, create culture shifts, capitalize on moments of opportunity, etc., the pacesetting leader must also know when to slow down, assess, consolidate, and check on culture metrics. Arguably, even high-performance teams should do this when needed, otherwise even the best can burn out. We have probably all served with pacesetting leaders who started fast and never slowed down, despite even being warned by other leaders. When the wheels begin to come off and pacesetting leadership is not adjusted, the pacesetting leader typically blames others for the lack of the team's performance. This is why pacesetting leadership, while good at the right time and place, is a dissonant leadership style. If used incorrectly it creates greater dissonance than resonance. The path of a pacesetting leader who fails to adjust leaves a wake of destroyed personnel and organizational resources. A pacesetting leader who uses this style judicially assesses the risk and reward, their teams' capabilities, and knows when to switch gears.

The second dissonant style is commanding leadership. Commanding leadership provides clarity, purpose, and direction in the midst of crisis. Highly effective during acute situations, commanding leadership keep people alive in combat, executes hard decisions in the board room, and is generally respected for decisiveness and decision-making. I have seen this countless times on the battlefield and in the boardroom. However, commanding leadership has detrimental effects if used over the long term.[53] Every situation in life is not a crisis or a life-or-death decision. A commanding leadership style when used in and of itself in nearly every situation prohibits creative thinking, diminishes space for democratic leadership to develop a comprehensive plan, disregards affiliative leadership, drives relentless vision without building trust and buy in, and directs and demands instead of empowering others by coaching. Or, maybe you've not shaken off the day as a professional leader and arrived home still in the role of executive, commander, or boss. Your significant other or family bears the brunt of your commanding presence, much to the detriment of everyone. In today's remote and hybrid workplace, where employees value autonomy and creative space, commanding leaders struggle to establish a locus of control, and should consider implementing other leadership styles. Commanding leadership can be used passionately and purposefully, but it must be used with precision, sparingly, otherwise it will create a toxic, unproductive culture of broken trust.

We teach Goleman's emotional intelligence theory and leadership styles in our Vanguard XXI leadership development and executive coaching courses two-fold. For leaders to gain a greater awareness of themselves, and for coaches to effectively use EQ assessments and tools as part of their executive leadership coaching practice.

Goleman's work is reflected in Korn Ferry's Emotional and Social Competency Inventory (ESCI), a comprehensive emotional intelligence analysis tool for the purposes of coaching leaders and teams. Peers, subordinates, and direct reports fill out a battery of questions qualified and quantified by the four EQ domains as well as giving written feedback. As a Korn Ferry certified facilitator of the ESCI, we use it as integral element of our International Coaching Federation (ICF) leadership coaching curriculum and in our own executive coaching with clients. It provides leaders with holistic feedback to their leadership styles and aids in better understanding the context and implementation of high-performance leadership.

[53] Goleman, Boyatzis, and McKee, Primal Leadership. 21.

You Mean I Can Learn This Stuff?

When I taught transformational moral leadership (ethics) in the Army, we could not secure the funding to provide every young officer—lieutenants and captains—in their respective basic and advanced courses a Korn Ferry ESCI, despite my best efforts. So, I built a tool based off my research, writing, and the basic known competencies and attributes of EQ. The tool was intuitive and allowed for bias, which proved helpful. Every student identified their primary and secondary EQ leadership style on the form. Then they evaluated themselves on a scale of one to five of how well they practiced each of the twelve EQ attributes. Here's the fun part. They then passed it to the five to six other officers in their squad who trained with them every day for the six-month course. Each officer provided their own feedback, being capable of seeing the other scores.

The results and feedback were astounding. The candor and respect students offered one another, girded with a growth mindset to seek self-improvement and encourage others to improve as they will serve and fight alongside one another, was impressive to witness. We then had a discussion in small and large group settings about the findings. We even conducted a controlled study with the Army Research Institute (ARI) among hundreds of officer candidate students to verify our process.

One day a young West Point lieutenant came up to me after class. He excitedly showed me his assessment, proclaiming that he had scored a majority of "one" in every category of EQ attributes. I kindly reminded him that was the lowest possible score out of five. He acknowledged my point, saying that was what he was excited about. I was confused, so he explained. He was one of a handful of new second lieutenants who had the opportunity to attend US Army Ranger School before attending Infantry Officer Basic Course (IBOLC). You can fail Ranger School for a myriad of reasons. Typically, the big three are: "patrols" (i.e., not mastering the tactics, techniques, or leadership of conducting missions), physical injury, and peer evaluations (when your peers "peer you out" for not being a trusted agent and team player). This young man had been "peered out."

Now, sitting in his IBOLC class, he once again received consistently low feedback regarding his EQ, and it was an eye-opening experience. The attributes that peered him out in Ranger School were the same attributes he received low scores for from yet another peer group in another course. He asked me one question.

"Sir, can I learn EQ?"

I acknowledged that he could, with practice, and he was elated. He then shared his excitement saying that if he could learn EQ then he could return to Ranger School and graduate, become a better Army officer, and enrich overall relationships in his life. The power of the EQ360, when utilized and properly coached, is a game changer for leaders. For this young man—who received a $400,000 West Point education with a five-year commitment of service to the Army following graduation—quite possibly changed the course of his professional development.

Tweet It

I've never been a tweeter, or on Twitter (now X). However, there is something very powerful about Twitter's initial attempt at condensing a thought process to one hundred and forty characters or less. Today, it's two hundred and eighty, but I'm not certain that increases the quality of what is tweeted. The thought process is powerful when related to how leaders clearly convey their leadership philosophy. I first began using this tool about ten years ago to help military leaders condense their "command philosophy" briefs from several dozen PowerPoint slides to something that would stick with soldiers at any rank.

The power of conveying and being held accountable to a 140-character leadership philosophy was on full display with the 2016-2017 number one ranked NCAA DIV I Gonzaga men's basketball team. On a beautiful fall September weekend in 2016, I had the privilege of leading this team through a leadership development and coaching retreat in the woods of Farragut State Park. It went so well, two years later I had the opportunity to do it again with the Baylor men's basketball team who went on to win the Big 12 that year, and a national championship the following season.

At the conclusion of the weekend, I instructed the players to "tweet" their personal 140-character leadership philosophy, based upon everything they had learned that weekend. I assumed they would use their individual workbooks provided for the weekend's events. I was wrong, forgetting I was working with Gen Y. What happened next was incredible. Each player took to their twitter handles and shared with the world their individual leadership philosophy. It caught on like wildfire. Their collective tweets were retweeted upwards of fifty thousand times in the next twenty-four hours and inspired the Zags nation. Ownership drives accountability, and accountability drives ownership. That team rallied around one word for the whole season, "sacrifice." It was an honor to share that journey with them, to include traveling to the Final Four to see their climatic and heartbreaking end losing to UNC Chapel Hill in the National Championship Game in Phoenix, AZ. Today, multiple players from that team, to include bench players, have played or continue to play in the NBA.

Reflect on what you've discovered in this book and who you are, how you think, and how you lead. What is your leadership philosophy? Try and tweet it—one hundred and forty characters or less. Practice excellence and avoid the two hundred and eighty.

M's British Bulldog

In the James Bond movie *Skyfall*, Bond mocks MI-6's leader, M, for her ceramic British Bulldog that sits atop her desk. When terrorists destroy MI-6, it is the only artifact from M's office that survives. At the end of the movie, Bond is gifted the bulldog from M's personal assistant, Money Penny, as a token to remember her by. This is called a leadership relic. A picture, image, object, quote, something of significance that a leader displays in a prominent location defining who they are, how they think, and how they lead. It tells a powerful story. It conveys truth. It provides transparency and insight into the leader and purpose, distance, and direction for those they lead.

My leadership relic is a four-sided wooden shepherd's crook given to me by a team of Ranger Chaplains and Religious Affairs Specialists at the Airborne and Ranger Training Brigade (ARTB) as a departing gift, having served two and a half years as the Brigade Chaplain. The top of the crook has my name emblazoned into the wood, and on reverse side a Ranger Tab epoxied into the staff. Emblazoned down each side of the staff are the titles "Ranger," "Pastor," "Priest," and "Prophet," each followed by a scripture verse. When they presented the staff to me, they explained that I had served them as their shepherd through emulating the four roles and responsibilities listed and had taught and trained them to serve the same as chaplains. It was a significant emotional event.

I was filled with gratitude, humility, and joy. What they didn't know was the significance of my last name "Randall." Our name traces back to roughly the fifteenth century middle Saxony in England, although it was spelled differently back then, Wrenwolf, which meant, "runner of wolves" or "Ring/Shield." My family origin comes from a tribe of shepherds. But no ordinary shepherds. Our shepherd tribe hunted down wolf packs and killed them before they ever got to the sheep. My eighth great grandfather was a Massachusetts militiaman at the Lexington and Concord skirmishes against the British Army, initiating the shot heard around the world declaring American Independence. My fifth great grandfather, also a Massachusetts infantryman, was captured by the Confederacy and held as a POW during the American Civil War in pursuit of unifying a nation, upholding all people are created equal with a right to flourish.

Generations have served since then. I served for over twenty years, my daughter serves today, and one of my sons plans to serve. Yes, relics mean something. My relic represents my leadership philosophy to promote human flourishing, transform leaders, and forge excellence through moral courage, moral reasoning, and moral leadership, and empower people to practice excellence. To protect the innocent, free the oppressed, and pursue and punish the oppressor.

What is *your* leadership relic? Was it given to *you* by someone else? Did you create it or find it? What story does it tell?

Coaching Subordinates, Peers, and Leaders

The final exercise for leaders is to take their 140-character tweet, consider their relic, and write a one-page executive summary on their leadership philosophy. The thesis statement is a leader's tweet. Just like good ole fashioned English 101, they write an intro paragraph, three body paragraphs, and a conclusion. The three body paragraphs reflect on how they practice excellence in who they are, how they think, and how they lead. The conclusion provides an opportunity to the reader to hold them accountable and take ownership and for the reader to know how they will be held accountable by the leader. It serves as an excellent initial counseling, coaching, or Individual Development Plan (IDP) or leadership development tool.

When in supervisory and leadership roles, I share mine with those I am privileged to lead, serve with as peers, and who I serve as a trusted leader. EQ leaders are leaders of influence who influence influential leaders. EQ leaders demonstrate self-awareness, transparency, authenticity, empathy, and a growth mindset to grow themselves and those in their sphere of influence. EQ leaders practice who they are, how they think, and how they lead. They contemplate how effectively they lead as thought leaders and how they influence thought leaders in their space. EQ leaders improve and grow their EQ attributes and gain confidence and capability in leading with all six EQ leadership styles at the right time, place, and with the right people. They acknowledge and accept that who they are as a trusted leader of character, and how they think critically exponentially shapes how they lead.

What has shifted for you in what it means to practice excellence using EQ leadership? Where do you need to grow in your EQ? What EQ leadership styles do you rely on most? Which ones do you want to practice and implement into your leadership? How can the process of developing a tweet, a relic with a story behind it, and an executive leadership summary transform your leadership development and coaching process?

Ready? Tweet it. Tell it. Transcribe it.

··· Chapter Nine: Practicing Excellence and Finishing Well, Trusted Agents & Trusted Leaders

Give thanks to the Lord, for he is good; his love endures forever, Let the redeemed of the Lord tell their story. – Psalms 107:1-2

In a temporal world filled with immediate gratification, what does it mean to practice excellence and finish well? As I already mentioned, I was a third alternate to receive an appointment to West Point. I struggled academically, failed a class, toyed with a 2.0 GPA for the first couple of years, to go on to graduate on the Dean's list my last three semesters. I spent one hundred and twenty days in Army Ranger School, a 62-day course, recycled two phases, and finally graduated. When I showed up to Ft. Bragg (now Ft. Liberty), North Carolina in 1997, I was full of ambition, initiative, and hopefulness in an aspiring Army career. The first two years were awesome, in my mind. Leadership development is an ongoing process, and I had a lot to learn. Hopefully this book shares some insights that you can benefit from far sooner than I did in my leadership career (as my younger 22-year-old self would have), wherever you are on your own leadership journey.

On paper, things looked good for me, back then. I was fortunate to serve as a platoon leader for two years, in a line platoon and a specialty platoon. That's a compliment in the Army as a young lieutenant, rather than being moved quickly to a staff position. I became a jumpmaster—the guy who exits paratroopers out the door of an aircraft. I completed a six-month deployment to the Middle East. As a senior first lieutenant, I had submitted my packet to attend the Special Forces Assessment and Selection Course, a pre-requisite for the Special Forces Qualification "Q" Course to become a Green Beret.

One cool January evening in 1999, flying at one hundred and thirty knots at eight hundred feet above the ground in a C-130, I conducted my final "clear to the rear" maneuver as a jumpmaster, grabbing the sides of the open aircraft door with my hands, arms extended, in a deep front stance, bracing myself as I hung my body out of the aircraft to observe the drop zone and trail aircraft. Basically, imagine hanging out the passenger door of a perfectly good airplane, only holding on by your hands. When I came back into the aircraft, I felt fine. When I landed, it was a different story. Following a twelve-mile road march back to our unit area, I went home and couldn't see very well. I had not worn eye protection on the jump, and unbeknownst to me, a blast of air had detached my retina. I could only see a kaleidoscope of colors out of my left eye, essentially blind. I was rushed into surgery and during pre-op it was discovered that I also had not one, but two inguinal hernias. I panicked. My Army career as a Paratrooper, Ranger, and hopefully Special Forces was flashing right before my eyes—both my good eye and my bad eye!

The next forty-five days included multiple surgeries and put me on medical convalescent leave for several months. I missed my SFAS date. My commander determined me "no longer fit to be a Paratrooper," and tried to put me on orders to report to Korea less than thirty days after my first surgery, while still on convalescent leave. Empathy wasn't a leadership attribute in the 1990s.

I grew angry and bitter at the Army, my leadership, and God. What was happening? Why did I deserve this? What was going to happen next? Fortunately, three of our senior leaders in the battalion came to my defense and convinced the commander to allow me to stay in the unit as a staff officer. Physically, I was present, but mentally and emotionally the event led me to check out and look for what was next. The next two years, I made my plan to leave the Army after my five-year commitment to pursue the corporate world.

And that new life seemed awesome. My wife and I were making six figures a year and living on a golf course. I had a great job, amazing boss (we are still friends today), and met some wonderful co-workers, one who I sit on a board with today. But internally, I wasn't happy. I left the profession of arms, a profession and tribe of people I dearly loved. Exactly one hundred days after I left the Army, terrorists struck the United States on 9/11. A few months after that, still angry at the Army and God, and unsatisfied in my new world, I found myself on the floor of my home office weeping uncontrollably for hours on end one night. Prostrate on the floor, I exhausted myself. I could not be consoled until I let go of my pain and gave it to God.

In the spring of 2002, God gave me an idea for a book on principled centered leadership. I wrote it and started a small leadership consulting company on the side. Small gigs, occasional speaking and training opportunities. But it just didn't feel right. Better, but not the "best." Pretty good, but not excellent. What *was* going excellent was my walk with God. I was deeply journaling, studying, praying, and active in my faith community. There was clarity. My heart and mind were open to hear from God.

Then, that fall, my wife woke me up from my sleep. She said I was laughing out loud and asked what I was dreaming about. I paused, hesitant to tell her. I asked her if God had revealed anything to her in prayer or study. She said he had, and that I was supposed to return to the Army. I was stunned, afraid, and excited all at once. I shared with her that God had told me the same thing, except for one significant change. He was calling me to full-time ministry to serve as an Army Chaplain. She affirmed the calling and said it was the best decision I had made thus far. I replied it was the first time in my life I was not making my own decisions, instead I was one hundred percent surrendering my life to God's plan for me.

Soon after, we sold everything we owned (losing money on our house), we returned to our hometown of Denver, Colorado, to live in a one-bedroom apartment. We somehow managed to survive on my wife's private school income of $18,000 a year, an eighty-five percent reduction in income, so I could attend Denver Seminary and volunteer as a police chaplain. When we became pregnant, I needed a source of income as my wife planned to stay home with our child. We needed a new plan.

The following summer I received a phone call from a local pastor after he read my book (to this day we cannot understand how he ordered it off my website that had been shut down for over a year). He asked me to be the keynote speaker at his denominations pastor leadership conference. I spoke on leadership and used a video clip with profanity in it, and he approached me afterwards to ask if I would like a job at the church. I accepted, not knowing what kind of job he was offering me. He then explained to me that he would appreciate my leadership as his administrative pastor and conference administrator. If I wanted to become a chaplain, I needed to first know how to be a pastor … and he offered to teach me. Today, I am eternally grateful to Pastor Dennis Jeffery, a spiritual mentor and father to me.

We returned to active duty on June 1st, 2006, ten years to the day I graduated from West Point and five years to the day I had left the Army … angry, bitter, and lost. I returned to active duty with a renewed sense of excellence with aligned passion, purpose, and precision. God clearly called me to serve in the role of shepherd. Over the next fifteen years, God provided me the opportunity to serve in every conventional and special operations unit I ever wanted to serve in as a shooter. It was God's more excellent way that I humbly served those shooters as their shepherd. Now, that kind of transformation isn't easy. You can put the chaplain into the Ranger, but it's hard to take the Ranger out of the chaplain. I wrestled with this for a few years. Over time, I found that most leaders wrestle with such a shift in passion, purpose, or precision. A growth mindset and disciplined obedience brings alignment over time to practice excellence.

Sometimes "Ranger Randall" led with more intensity than what some may expect from a chaplain. Other times, "Chaplain Randall" led with more compassion and empathy than required out of an abundance of the heart. Transformation takes time. Through spiritual contemplation, spiritual mentors, and real-world experiences, I transitioned from a dichotomy of the two personas to a holistic identity aligning my passion, purpose, and precision. It led me to an embrace a philosophy of who I truly am as a chaplain. It's four-fold: pastor, priest, prophet, person. I believe this four-fold identity defines what it means to be a chaplain. I knew this philosophy had become my spiritual praxis when the Ranger chaplains presented me with that shepherd's crook.

Full-time professional chaplains likely experience the wholeness of human flourishing and suffering more than any of the four individual roles, responsibilities, and identities combined. It's not a competition or comparison; instead, it's the journey of the profession. Transformational leaders learn to maintain presence—whether by elongating or shortening spans of time—and see that periods of transition between events are just as important as the event itself. Transformational leaders learn to utilize different leadership styles, no different than how clergy must learn how to transition to different ministry styles. Transitioning one's heart, head, and hands from pastor, to priest, to prophet, to person sometimes happens quickly. It's not systematic, linear, or mutually exclusive. The identities mutually support one another, submitting to the one with the right intent, at the right time and place while serving those present with excellence.

I will always remember the night I provided a chapel service at a small outstation dining facility in Afghanistan. I preached on Romans 12:1-2, the passage where the Apostle Paul expounds on being a living sacrifice and being transformed by the renewing of our minds versus being conformed by the things of this world. One of our special operators stuck around afterwards. We ate ice cream and celebrated his thirtieth birthday. We discussed his sense of calling to leave his current profession and become an Army chaplain. Eighteen hours later, his teammates and I held hands, prayed together, and then zipped up his body bag. A copy of his notes from chapel, which he had tucked into his Bible, are framed in my office today. He had taken away three points that day. His calling to be a warrior. He must train at it every day. He asked God to draw him closer to his presence than he had ever been before. Passion. Purpose. Precision.

I will always remember a hot July Friday afternoon at a small country church with several hundred friends, family, unit members, and a solemn graveside, as I presided over the funeral of one of our special operators. As we left the ceremony, the Army Special Operations Commander and his Command Chaplain both presented me with coins of "excellence" for the event, which was only successful due to a team of people working together to honor a fallen teammate. I appreciated the gesture but forgot the coins in my truck console until sometime later. More importantly, for myself and several dads, we had less than an hour to change clothes, pick up our daughters, and drive for several hours to our unit's Father & Daughter Weekend Retreat, that I was also facilitating. I'll always remember that drive, working through the emotions and mindset of transitioning from a place of grief and suffering while providing that priestly presence, to a jovial and energetic pastor, friend, and dad. I somehow managed to effectively facilitate that weekend of fun and connection between dads and their children, something our fallen comrade, Ben, would never do again.

I will always remember the discreet conversations with combat leaders. On one hand, exercising pastoral care and empathy for their combat losses while also embracing their anger for the enemy, and grief for the lost. At the same time, wearing the prophetic hat, reminding them of what they can and cannot control, and holding the moral and ethical tension to ensure that their decisive actions are aligned with their personal moral compass and ethics of our military profession.

I will also always remember, as a senior pastor, celebrating in worship with families at chapel and rejoicing for an upcoming childbirth, to holding a stillborn baby in my arms grieving with two young parents the following week and officiating the subsequent funeral.

I will always remember the requests by warriors for "one of those Ranger Chaplain prayers," as helicopter blades whirl above, producing a static electricity "green halo" seen under night vision goggles or the smell of engine exhaust and hum of vehicle engines, and giving communion on the floor of a helicopter just before takeoff. Soldiers locked arm in arm while I invoked passages of scripture, empowering God's protection and authorizing just and righteous responses to those who oppress and do evil.

I will always remember my own prayers over the same men and women as I rode and walked with them on combat patrols.

I will always remember the humor of praying before any airborne operation, reminding paratroopers that as a chaplain I will happily pray for them on the ground, but once we get in the aircraft, I start praying for myself, too, because we all have the same government issued parachute.

I will always remember facilitating dozens of weekend marriage and family retreats, while balancing the role of facilitator to the dozens of couples and families, remaining present as a husband and father to my wife and family, and serving as pastor and person to all.

It was in these environments, working with high performance individuals involved in some of the nation's most pressing missions, that I began to develop today's Vanguard leadership development and coaching model, the Vanguard Way. Through these opportunities I was afforded the opportunity to spend eight years in Major League Baseball, two years in NCAA Division I basketball, attend graduate and postgraduate school, and develop and teach transformational leadership and ethics for the Army's officer and non-commissioned officer corps.

In September 2014, I was sitting outside of PNC Park preparing a chapel message for the Pittsburgh Pirates and visiting team. I had just finished reading a book, *Leaders Who Last*, by Dave Kraft. And for the first time since that night in 2002, I distinctly heard God pressing me on my calling again. His new mission? To be an influential leader to influential leaders. What has followed over the last ten years is fully stepping into the marketplace as a thought leader in leadership development and executive coaching. Throughout these experiences I began investing in more mentoring relationships and surrounding myself with influential leaders of character who provided mentorship, counsel, coaching, accountability, and ownership.

So, let's return to the question I asked at the beginning of the chapter. In a temporal, immediately gratifying world, what does it mean to finish well?

Finishing well requires running the race with trusted agents and fellow leaders of character. Please take a moment and read the acknowledgements at the end of this book. I can count each of these leaders of character as trusted agents who have poured and continue to pursue excellence together in life. We cannot pursue excellence alone. If you wrote a book about your life, who would be in your acknowledgement section?

Practicing excellence requires finding Aristotle's mean, the center of his circle. It is pursuing the Apostle Paul's more excellent way. Practice makes permanent, so what we practice must be done with passion, purpose, and precision. However, sometimes that practice and process can look messy ... because it is. Practice does not make perfect. We find that ultimate alignment of passion, purpose, and precision when we pursue the heart of God and discover who we are and whose we are. That is why the Psalmist proclaims the "redeemed of the Lord tell their story." Because God has redeemed what they may have compromised themselves in their own fallible minds, ambitions, and desires.

What are you practicing today that is considered excellent? Who are you seeking out and giving permission to join you?

Trusted Agents of Character and Circles of Trust

Here are three exercises you may find helpful to answer these questions. The first exercise is based upon the sociological human relationships that create holistic wellness. Write your name in the center of the exercise. Next write as many names as possible in each circle you like. It may also be helpful to circle or highlight the "go to" person in that circle.

PE: Coaching Tool
Developing Transformational Trusted Relationships

When filling out these exercises, a few realizations may come to mind. First, very few can fill out all these circles completely at any given time in the journey to excellence. However, over time, we can become more proficient at pursuing and creating these essential relationships in our life.

Second, yes, you *can* have the same person in multiple circles, however, there is a cost. Have you asked them permission? Do they know that is what you are asking of them? Have you asked them to fulfill many areas of your life where someone else may be more suited, capable, and fulfilled? So, if your spouse or significant other is in every circle, go apologize and ask where they most love to walk with you on the journey.

Third, no, you shouldn't put yourself in these circles. I once had a professional sports coach fill this out. He wrote "me" in every circle. When I challenged him on it, he explained how successful he was, how he had arrived at this point on his own hard work, and how he didn't trust or need anyone else.

"How's that working out for you?" I asked him.

"I guess that's why management has me talking to you," he replied. Maybe.

We coached together and pursued trusted relationships. Today, he is incredibly successful in his industry, with a robust circle of trusted relationships that grow, protect, and support him.

From a professional angle, the following two exercises may be helpful in assessing how you lead as a trusted agent of character to leaders you work for, and how you as a leader surround yourself with trusted agents of character.

How do you give and receive advice?

First, develop a list of those to whom you serve as a trusted advisor. Typically, the "Leader as Trusted Agent" in Illustration I is your boss or who you directly report to. In Illustration II , place yourself in the center circle, "Leader's Trusted Agents," and develop a list of those from whom you receive advice from. Complete the first exercise, then move on to the second exercise.

Trusted moral agents typically serve in one or more roles as experienced, experts, coaches, mentors, professional friends, and confidential advisors.[54] The first exercise considers an understanding of how a trusted professional as a leader can effectively serve as a trusted advisor to senior leaders. Consider where you most enjoy functioning as a leader for the leader you report to. We all have a wheelhouse we prefer. Prioritize the four circles 1-4, recognizing that all four circles are connected with a ring, because for many leaders we move into different roles based upon what is required of us.

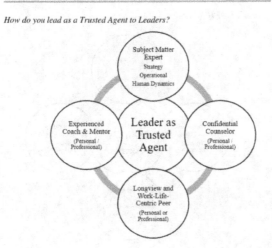

PE: Coaching & Being Coached
Taking Advice & Trusted Advisors

How do you lead as a Trusted Agent to Leaders?

Subject Matter
Expert
Strategy
Operational
Human Dynamics

Experienced
Coach & Mentor
(Personal /
Professional)

Leader as
Trusted
Agent

Confidential
Counselor
(Personal /
Professional)

Longview and
Work-Life-
Centric Peer
(Personal or
Professional)

Now, consider where your boss most utilizes you. Label the circles again in order A-D. What have you discovered? Typically, if 1-4 is aligned with A-D you probably enjoy showing up every day and working with your leader. Why? Because they draw the most potential out of you in the area in which you are most qualified, confident, and comfortable.

However, if 1-4 and A-D are misaligned, what does that reveal to you? It may reveal why you show up every day and go home every day

---

[54] Dan Ciampa, *Taking Advice: How Leaders Get Good Advice and Use it Wisely* (Boston: Harvard Business Review, 2006), 107.

frustrated, anxious, stressed, and unfulfilled. What if your leader seeks out someone else in your wheelhouse? How does that impact your relationship with that subordinate leader at work? What if your leader is asking you to function in one or more areas that is not your wheelhouse? How does this exercise create a positive and growing coaching conversation with your leader and how the two of you show up, work, and lead together every day?

PE: Coaching & Being Coached
Taking Advice & Trusted Advisors

Who are your Trusted Agents?

Subject Matter Expert
Strategy
Operational
Human Dynamics

Experienced Coach & Mentor
(Personal / Professional)

Leader's Trusted Agents

Confidential Counselor
(Personal / Professional)

Longview and Work-Life-Centric Peer
(Personal or Professional)

In my experience as a staff officer, leadership coach, and subordinate leader, I have found times where I am asked to serve in one or more of these areas whether they are my preferred wheelhouse in that role or not. What's most important is understanding how the leader you serve is asking you to lead. Sometimes I've been the subject matter expert on world religions, ethics, or leadership. Other times, I've been the executive coach or mentor. Some leaders—because we have similar backgrounds—rely on me for a professional friendship, and at times other leaders seek me out as a confidential counselor.

The second exercise challenges you, the leader, to consider who you have chosen as trusted advisors. This tends to be the harder exercise. Sometimes leaders realize they have too many people acting as trusted advisors who do not meet the requirements to be one. Often, leaders are missing essential trusted advisors capable of coaching and mentoring them to lead well and avoid moral and ethical failures. Similar to the first exercise focused on our personal lives, this exercise helps leaders assess where their leadership "gaps" are in a professional setting, and how they may consider building trust with subordinate leaders to fill those gaps.

In a military setting, this includes a conversation regarding how commanders could and should utilize their chaplain as a confidential counselor, moral ethical advisor, and spiritual leader. Professional chaplains in the military, professional sports, hospital, law enforcement, or corporate marketplace are most effective when they understand their role is four-fold as a pastor, priest, prophet, and person. Knowing what role to fulfill is based upon understanding what that leader and organization most need at any given moment on any given day.

When I look back at my 28-year leadership journey, regardless of the joy or suffering, mountain top or valley, God has always been there, and he has always provided friends and leaders along the journey. We were not created or destined to live this life alone. We were created for relationships. A vertical relationship with our Creator and Savior, and horizontal relationships with family, friends, and trusted leaders of character.

Practicing excellence is an art and science that requires a lifetime to seek fulfilled. Every breath we breathe provides us another opportunity to practice living a life more abundant to fulfill our passion and purpose, and experience joy in the precision of who we are, how we think, and what we do. As we finish our time together on this journey of practicing excellence, pause and reflect on these key questions as you consider who you are, how you think, how you lead, and what your life looks like practicing excellence.

Who are you?
> *Who are you as a person of trusted character?*
> *What virtues define you?*
> *What are your pillars of virtue to lead from with excellence?*
> *What are your vices requiring change and growth?*

How do you think?
> *What is your decision-making process?*
> *What are your moral values that are non-negotiable?*
> *What are your ethical values that are non-negotiable?*
> *Where is there alignment? If not, what must change?*

How do you lead?
> *What is your leadership philosophy? Can you "tweet" it in 140 characters or less?*
> *What is your one-page leadership philosophy executive summary? How will you use it?*
> *What is your relic that defines you and helps you tell your story?*

How will you practice excellence?
> *How do you define excellence?*
> *What is your passion (calling)?*
> *How will you be purposeful in using your gifts and skills? (What are they?)*
> *Where will you lead with precision (your marketplace)?*
> *What are your next steps to practicing excellence?*

The Apostle Paul writes, "Not that I have already obtained all this, or have already arrived at my goal; but I press on to take hold of that for which Christ Jesus took hold of me." (Phil 3:12) And, "For now I will show you a more excellent way." (1 Corinthians 12:31)

May I encourage you on your journey of practicing excellence that practice makes permanent, it is a constant journey, and there is a more excellent way by loving God and loving people.

··· Epilogue

The white belt mentality has led me through life to consistently invest in the art of practice facilitating the opportunity to achieve results when it counts. Gen. Daniel Allyn, former Vice Chief of Staff of the Army, once said, "You can't surge character." How you show up every single day is in direct correlation to how you practice in the moment, and in the moments to come.

Today, Vanguard XXI and our Vanguard Way, transforms leaders and forges excellence in individuals and organizations due to hundreds of years of combined experience, practice, and application from our world class team of leaders and coaches. We have learned from our failures and success. We have found joy and struggle in the art of practicing excellence. We have a true and tested process providing a transformational experience for leaders from all battlefields, boardrooms, marketplaces, public squares, and walks of life. Regardless of the environment, we find fulfillment empowering leaders to win.

I've always enjoyed leadership from owning my own paper route at eleven years old to becoming an Eagle Scout and team captain in high school sports. West Point taught me the principles of what is required to become a leader of character. Through more trial and error as a young officer, from how I led and what I observed from other leaders, I began to learn the difference between productive and unproductive leadership. We used to call that toxic leadership until recently, but it was deemed too harsh by society. My question is, for who? Those experiencing toxic leadership still pay the price, regardless of what it's called. And the toxic leader typically gets promoted because they excel at skills and know how to get results. We teach, train, coach, and practice a better, transformational way.

I used to share with young lieutenants and captains that Lieutenant Colonel Randall in 2019 had a whole list of discussion points for 2nd Lieutenant Randall of 1997. Isn't that true for all of us, to some degree, when we choose a white belt mentality? Hopefully, we've all grown in who we are, how we think, and how we lead. Hopefully, today as leaders we have a stronger epistemological approach to empowering people and promoting human flourishing. To be influential thought leaders we must think epistemologically and transform the thinking of influential leaders. To do that we must break the bell curve of mediocrity believing practice makes permanent, therefore ensuring our practice is passionate, purposeful, and precise.

My journey in leadership development and theology began to finely intertwine on a mess hall napkin in Iraq in 2007. Amid combat deployments, I desired to develop a process that would strengthen a soldier holistically spiritually, physically, mentally, relationally, and as a leader. I began to teach it, and by 2008 it grew into a concept, which was shared by a couple of my mentors with the higher echelons of the Army Chaplain Corps and the Department of the Army. It caught the attention of our Chief of Chaplains, a two-star general. He requested I speak at the 2009 chaplain senior leadership conference for lieutenant colonels, colonels, and general officers. The result? A few weeks before my speaking engagement, a chaplain, colonel in rank, who worked in the Pentagon called me and accused me of plagiarism. When I asked what his proof was, he simply looked at me.

"You're only a captain, chaplain. You're not senior ranking or smart enough to develop something like this on your own."

Haters gonna hate ... even chaplains. The keynote speech went incredibly well along with a couple other speakers sharing about holistic health and fitness. I'm not sure how much my presentation impacted the Army in the end, however, between 2008 and 2013 the Army's Comprehensive Soldier Fitness program incorporating spiritual, social, physical, family, and emotional fitness came to life. It was the precursor to the Army's Health and Holistic Fitness (H2F) program today. I took those experiences with me to my years serving in the US Army's Special Operations Command where, through collaboration with other professionals in the chaplaincy, medical corps, sports psychologists, athletic trainers, and other holistic leaders, we developed and implemented processes to enhance soldiers and family's holistic wellness.

In 2011, I invited my good friend Dr. Nate Zinnser, who after thirty years recently retired from West Point's Center for Enhanced Performance, to come speak to our SOF operators on the high-performance mental game. "Doc Z," as he's affectionately called, was my sports psychologist when I was a collegiate athlete at the Academy. He helped me win a national championship. More importantly, he helped me learn how to study, handle stress, and pass my classes so I could graduate! Doc has worked with thousands of Army athletes, Olympians, and professional athletes, to include Eli Manning. (He's a legend.) Thirty-two years later, he and I partner together working with high performance teams in leadership development, coaching, and human performance. He's Yoda, while I'm still a Jedi in training. It's good to be a Jedi when you have a Jedi Master.

Doc couldn't attend, so he recommended I reach out to one of the up and coming (and today one of the leading mental conditioning coaches in sports psychology and professional sports) Dr. Bernie Holliday. Bernie worked with Doc at USMA and recently had been hired by the Pittsburgh Pirates as their Mental Conditioning Director. Bernie and I quickly aligned, having both trained with Doc, and he asked if he could also bring the Pirates Assistant GM, Kyle Stark to our training. Kyle and Neal Huntington, the Pirates General Manager, had brought a winning philosophy from the Cleveland Indians (now Guardians) based upon character development and talent to the Pirates, subsequently hiring Clint Hurdle, one of the "winningest" Skippers in Major League Baseball, as Manager. Collectively, with a world class front office, team of coaches, player development, and support staff, took the Pirates to the playoffs three years in a row from 2013-2015 after a twenty-year absence. They were one of the "winningest" baseball teams during that decade, even though they had one of the smallest budgets in MLB. They won with character and leadership development, talent management, and coaching.

Kyle and Bernie crushed it with our guys. Their blend of high-performance sports psychology and leadership development, based upon assessing character and talent, won the day. While with our unit, they also observed some teaching and training I provided on spiritual leadership, holistic fitness, and family wellness. The military and professional sports are very similar in time spent away from loved ones, multiple family moves, and performing at peak levels as a professional under a myriad of stress and pressure. Kyle asked if I would like to join the team as a chaplain and provide some leadership coaching. I obliged and became, from what we know, the first ever internally hired chaplain for a team in the MLB. I was privileged to spend eight seasons with the Pirates family from 2013-2020. At that time, I also began providing leadership coaching. Stepping into this space, without any prior professional coaching experience, is what led me to begin pursuing professional coaching certification and training through the International Coaching Federation (ICF). I had over four thousand hours of counseling under my belt, but professional coaching is different. I had to stretch and grow. I didn't know what I didn't know.

Foundation, Growth, and Legacy

The Army sent me back to school earning a second master's degree and I began serving as the MCOE Ethics Instructor and Doctrine Writer from 2016 to 2019. My goal was to implement a comprehensive transformational moral leadership curriculum focused on character development, moral and ethical decision-making, emotional intelligence, and coaching. I also began seeking out individual coaching certifications and education leading me to my professional coaching credentials with the International Coaching Federation. Today, I'm an ICF PCC coach, working on my MCC credential, and have developed three ICF Coaching Certificate Courses.

We integrated basic coaching principles and transformational moral leadership together as a holistic leadership coaching process. Grounded in theological and philosophical concepts of human flourishing, we have found in historically prominent democratic nations, warrior classes, and warrior codes of excellence. The curriculum holistically teaches, trains, and coaches moral courage and character development, moral and ethical reasoning and decision-making, and moral empathy and emotionally intelligent leadership. One of our recent Vanguard Professional Coaching Course (VPCC) clients shared with me his leader's notebook from when he went through the command course as a colonel several years ago, that I taught. He shared with me the notes he took and applied while in command, and still applies in his leadership today.

Since students return every three to five years to the Army's PMEs, the goal was for the transformational moral leadership (TML) curriculum to provide an opportunity for self-reflection and self-assessment regarding one's own character development along Kohlberg's stages of psychological moral development. The students were also to consider how to teach and train character development with their additional education and experience when returning to their units.

Extraneously, a strategic goal was to experiment, validate, and master the curriculum for its eventual modification and implementation outside of the military in other professions seeking professional character development. We conducted several successful iterations with various Army special forces and conventional Army units and NCAA Division I college sports teams to include the 2016-2017 National Championship Runner Up Gonzaga men's basketball team and the 2018-2019 Baylor men's basketball team, who won the Big 12 conference that season and eventually won the national championship in 2020. Today, the curriculum is still being utilized in its third iteration with MCOE Ethics Instructors and SGIs.

The curriculum, as any good curriculum should, has been professionally enhanced and modified with each instructor ensuring the original foundational components align with current curriculum and student requirements. Since its inception in 2016 over forty thousand Army officer and non-commissioned officers (NCOs) have completed the training. My intent as the Ethics Instructor was to teach and train transformational moral leadership and character development to Army officers and NCOs. Additionally, I hoped to "train the trainer" and provide Professional Military Education (PMEs) and Small Group Instructors (SGI) training to teach the curriculum as well, thus creating a team of teams of Army leaders who embrace character development. This led to the development of the two-day Character Development Instructor Course (CDIC) for drill sergeants and SGIs, so they could conduct their own courses internal to their units.

In addition to classroom curriculum, the CDIC two-day experiential learning course implemented the six hours of TML curriculum into experiential learning environments including Olympic weightlifting, boxing and jiu-jitsu, and an obstacle course. Mental conditioning exercises based in sports psychology were incorporated into the obstacle course as well testing memory recall, breath control, meditation and relaxation techniques, communication, and teamwork under pressure of weight bearing load, agility, and time constraints.

The Myers-Briggs Type Indicator (MBTI) Conflict Style Report and the Korn Ferry ESCI emotional intelligence 360 assessment were utilized for psychological and behavioral type awareness and to gauge participants social/emotional intelligence. These courses created a holistic life-long learning strategy for successfully growing moral and ethical Army leaders. The TML curriculum included a robust list of books, periodicals, and videos for practitioners and students to read or watch before taking the courses. The training manual included PowerPoint, instructor notes, and classroom resources.

The TML curriculum was a comprehensive, holistic approach to teaching transformational moral leadership using David Kolb's Experiential Learning Cycle and theory. This theory uses concrete experiences, reflective observation, abstract conceptualization, and active experimentation to move students through a comprehensive learning process.[55]

Assessment of TML and CDIC

The CDIC began as a pilot program providing teaching and training for drill sergeants who train thousands of new recruits a year, and MCCC small group leaders who train several hundred senior first lieutenants and captains for Company Command. The two-day (eighteen hour) CDIC was completed by drill sergeants in a Brigade Combat Team (BCT) unit during the third quarter of fiscal year 2017. At the same time, the basic trainee attrition rate for this unit went from twelve percent in the third quarter down to three percent in the fourth quarter of fiscal year 2017, potentially saving the Army resources in terms of retaining recruits and impacting talent management. Additionally, it was directly correlated to reducing the number of drill sergeants under Army15-6 investigations for immoral and unethical behavior. Although correlational in nature, the unit's Command Sergeant Major attributed part of this success to drill sergeants applying what they learned in the CDIC. High performing trusted professionals and

---

[55] David A. Kolb, *Experiential Learning: Experience as the Source for Learning and Development* (Upper Saddle River, NJ: Pearson Education, 2015), 32.

leaders of character exponentially impact the teaching and training of future trusted professionals.

Over five hundred drill sergeants, MCCC Instructors, and Military Advisory Training Academy (MATA) instructors, and 7th Special Forces Group personnel completed the course between 2017 and 2020, all completing after action review (AAR) questionnaires, rating the quality of curriculum, instructor, and venue for each element of the course.

For evaluation purposes, a sample of ninety-three soldiers were selected to fill out the AAR based upon the audience and when the course was conducted over a longitudinal period of time from 2017 to 2020 to assess whether the integrity, efficacy, and value of the course was sustained over time in multiple training environments and among twelve different instructors. The participants were soldiers between the ages of eighteen to forty-five with one year to over twenty years of military service as enlisted, non-commissioned officers, and company and field grade officers. All participants have likely achieved a minimum of Kohlberg's Stage 2 of moral development, with the majority being in Stages 3 or 4, and a select few experienced leaders in Stage 5.

The purpose of the post-course survey was to measure participants' reactions to the course and participants' attitudes about character development. The responses were used to determine instructional quality of the CDIC and to provide recommendations to improve course training. Overall, the course surveys indicated that the training event was typically rated above standard. Participants commented on the quality of training, including material and content, instruction, and venue. Written comments indicated that participants thought the training was excellent, practical, and demanding.

Participants also indicated that they better understood themselves and others, intended to apply what they learned, and that others should attend similar training. Verbal comments regularly provided by the students consistently included that the CDIC was the best leadership course many senior NCOs and officers with over ten years of experience had every participated in during their time in the Army.[56]

Overall, this data constitutes initial evidence regarding the effectiveness of the approach, which is grounded in the MCOE's Human Performance Model (HPM) as a holistic attempt to develop the twenty-first century American soldier. To be the most cognitively dominant, realistically trained, and institutionally agile force in the world will require this type of development of strategic leadership and education across the Army.

I sought to integrate and collaborate with several key Army agencies for the curriculum. These agencies included the Center for the Army Professional Ethic (CAPE) and its strategic imperative to shape the Army Profession, the Army Chaplain Corps and its responsibility for moral leadership and ethics instruction, and the US Army Research Institute for the Behavioral and Social Sciences (ARI) and its role in the creation of assessments designed to support soldier development. ARI was incredibly collaborative and supportive. We worked together for three years teaching, training, and assessing the validity of the transformational leadership and character development program. We were fortunate to collectively capture and publish a professional article highlighting the three-year journey teaching and training over twelve thousand Army officers and non-commissioned officers, from the ranks of sergeant to lieutenant and captain, to lieutenant colonel and colonel. I had the unique opportunity to present our methodology at the US Army ethics conferences, international military ethics conferences, and travel oversees to work with the British Army and their ethicists.

In summary, for over three years we trained every Army Brigade Combat Team Infantry and Armor leader from platoon leader leading thirty to thirty-five person platoons to brigade commander leading formations three thousand to five thousand soldiers. This article provides a deep dive on our design, methodology, application, and results.

---

[56] CDIC After Action Reviews, internal document, 2017-2019.

Today, Vanguard XXI offers multiple International Coaching Federation (ICF) leadership development and coaching courses, such as ICF Level 1 and CCE courses as an ICF credentialed coaching academy. The Vanguard Way represents several iterations of transformation for leaders continually seeking growth, innovation, and improvement meeting the challenging demands of clients in today's VUCA world.

··· The Vanguard Way: A Trusted Leadership Development & Coaching Practice of Excellence

A vanguard is a military formation's lead unit. Vanguard organizations and leaders are at the forefront, the tip of the spear, those who engage the enemy or problem sets of their environment first. A vanguard forms, shapes, and creates space for the main force to accomplish its mission. The most successful vanguard units and leaders find their greatest success at the decisive moment was won in their relentless practice. I started Vanguard XXI in 2002 as a young 28-year-old corporate sales professional with five years of military service under my belt. To this day I enjoy keynote speaking, however, I wanted to go deeper after time on the stage to develop intentional relationships with leaders and their organizations.

My call into full-time ministry put my entrepreneurial aspirations to the side. God still had a plan; he just needed me to buy into it. For the next eighteen years, God provided incredible opportunities as I have shared in this book of going deeper through intentional relationship with leaders and organizations. I truly experienced what it meant to pursue epistemological thinking, human flourishing, and trusted relationships. Twenty-two years later, with the incredible teaching, training, and practice of Heroic Public Speaking and Mike and Amy Port, I've learned to share a transformational message that Mike and Amy believe can change the world, one keynote at a time. They constantly remind speakers and authors that a speech has the power to "change the world and the people in it, including the speaker."

My days with the Pittsburgh Pirates highlighted my need for continued teaching, training, and practice in professional coaching. Over the last several years, through a white belt mentality and growth mindset, I've pursued seven coaching certifications and hold an ICF PCC (Professional Certified Coach) credential. As I dove deeper into the world of professional coaching, it became evidently clear that the work we have done in the military and professional sports with transformational leadership could be combined with professional coaching.

Today's Vanguard Way, led by our team of professionals at the forefront of leadership development and coaching teach, train, coach, and practice our tried, true, and tested Vanguard process. Since 2021, we continue to improve our process training over three thousand leaders across diverse marketplaces from government to finance, military to manufacturing, professional sports to pharmaceuticals, and sales to software. I have personally taught, trained, or coached over fifteen thousand leaders with this transformative curriculum.

Vanguard XXI's leadership development model is designed for long-term partnership with organizations in each stage of individual and team development. As a full service, leadership development and coaching solution, our proven track record transforms leaders and organizations to operate as high character, high culture teams through our leadership development and coaching process. This powerful combination of teaching, training, and coaching facilitates dynamic, long-term transformational growth and results.

Today, this includes our signature Vanguard Professional Coaching Certification (VPCC). A sixty-one hour and an eighty hour International Coaching Federation Credentialed Level 1 Course. The VPCC is a holistic approach to teaching and coaching transformational leaders using David Kolb's Experiential Learning Cycle Theory. Using concrete experiences, reflective observation, abstract conceptualization, and active experimentation, participants engage in a comprehensive coaching and learning process.

The VPCC teaches and trains leaders how to coach and lead with high-performing, emotionally intelligent leadership as trusted advisors in today's VUCA (Volatile, Uncertain, Complex, and Ambiguous) world. It teaches the VXXI Coaching Model and process for how trusted professionals can lead, coach, plan, make decisions, execute, and drive results for those they coach and lead in today's present, hybrid, and remote global workplace environments. The VPCC emphasizes coaching and leadership modalities that build high character, high culture, high climate teams that attract, develop, and retain talent, thereby driving results. This includes character and psychological moral development, moral and ethical decision-making, and emotionally intelligent leadership practices.

Participants learn how to coach utilizing the Vanguard XXI Coaching Model. (See below) The course includes the Myers Briggs Conflict Style Report and the Korn Ferry EQ360 ESCI individual and group reports, providing student's psychological type theory and emotional intelligence 360 feedback on who they are, how they make decisions, and how they lead. It is optimal for individuals and organizations looking to certify coaches through the International Coaching Federation, the globally recognized gold standard for professional coaching. This course is also optimal for organizational leadership development and human resources leaders and teams, and internal and external coaching professionals. Vanguard XXI also partners with organizations to create their own internal coaching practices and program.

We offer a similar executive leadership course for c-suites, executive leadership teams, directors, managers, and supervisors, who are seeking to implement transformational leadership and a coaching culture and language to their organization. An industry leadership and coaching associate of mine, Tim Tiryaki, fondly reminds our space that "leadership development without coaching is just entertainment." I wholeheartedly agree. Tim and I have had the pleasure of working together, integrating leadership development and professional coaching into high performance organizations, such as the Joint Special Operations Command (JSOC). Individual, group, and team coaching are essential for achieving sustainable leadership development and growth in the breadth and depth of organizations.

In my experience, what I've found is that everyone needs a coach. Coaching is one of the four helping professions along with counseling, consulting, and mentoring. There are unique similarities and differences to each one that makes them unique and appropriate. Consider a basic x and y axis graph. The x axis represents who is leading the conversation, the counselor, consultant, mentor, coach, or the client. The y axis represents if the counselor, consultant, mentor, coach is providing more teaching, telling, and guidance, or taking a more curious posture and asking more powerful questions.

Counselors and consultants operate on the right side of the y axis leading their clients due to their expertise and training. Typically, people pursue a counselor because of their expertise in some sort of therapy practice, model, or practice that helps people reflect on their past issues, trauma, etc. and how to deal with it in the present and moving forward. Counselors lead the conversation as the therapist, asking powerful questions, and providing perspective and advice through the paradigm of a particular model or models of therapy. I have over four thousand and four hundred hours of counseling as a pastor and chaplain; helping people experiencing breakthrough is very rewarding.

Consultants are subject matter experts. They are highly-trained and educated in addition to life experience enabling them to identify problems, develop and implement solutions. Consultants lead their clients, teach and train their clients, and solve complex problems. Consultants may ask questions of clients to gain individual or institutional knowledge to solve problems. As subject matter experts, consultants are very effective at helping organizations become more efficient and effective in their marketplace.

Mentors and coaches shift to the opposite side of the y axis, where the client is leading the conversation and the mentor and coach follow. Mentoring is a sacred space. Have you ever been told by your organization that you were going to be placed in a mentor program and assigned a mentor? How did that work out for you? Forced mentoring programs are problematic for one main reason: the mentee is assigned a mentor with little choice on who it is.

Successful mentoring programs empower the mentee to choose the mentor. Why? Because mentoring is a sacred space. Mentoring is a process of pouring into a mentee, when that mentee has given them permission to do so, and that requires a trusted relationship. Mentors follow their clients, asking powerful questions with curiosity, engaged in who the mentee is, how they think, and how they act. Mentors answer mentees questions, and when given permission offer advice and counsel, maybe even some consulting, on ways a mentee can further develop and grow. Typically, a mentee chooses a mentor who they would like to emulate or experience similar success in life. The greatest mentor-mentee relationships follow the ancient principle that when the student is ready the teacher will appear.

Completing the four helping profession framework is coaching. Coaching in the purest sense partners "with the clients in a thought provoking and creative process that inspires them to maximize their personal and professional potential. The process of coaching often unlocks previously untapped sources of imagination, productivity, and leadership."[57]

In essence, great coaches coach people, not their problems. The more empowered a client becomes as a human being, flourishing in their potential, the greater control they have in life of solving their own problems. Coaching is the art of partnering and following the client, asking powerful questions and facilitating the client to grow. The ICF coaching models are built upon eight foundational competencies. They include demonstrating an ethical practice, embodying a coaching mindset, establishing and maintaining agreements, cultivating trust and safety, maintaining presence, active listening, evoking awareness, and facilitating client growth.

Coaches who seek to become ICF credentialed coaches must demonstrate varying degrees of mastery of these competencies at the ICF

---

[57] *https://coachingfederation.org/about*

ACC, PCC, and MCC levels of coaching. A typical coach pursues and completes this process in twelve to twenty-four months.

Reflecting on the four helping professions, take a few moments and conduct the following exercise to gain new self-awareness of how you utilize your skills as a leader. You can read more about the global success of coaching through the ICF here: *https://coachingfederation.org/research/global-coaching-study*

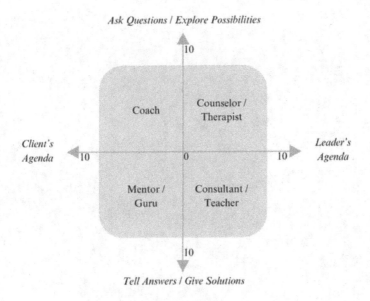

Today, we see organizations and leaders move to the vanguard of their marketplaces through leadership development and coaching as trusted character agents who align individual and collective passion, purpose, and precision in who they are, how they think, and how they lead. Individually and collectively, they learn and apply principles to transform leaders and forge excellence. As leadership trainers and executive coaches, we are humbled and privileged to be in the audience, celebrating transformational leaders and coaches win, on their stage.

We look forward to joining you and your organization in the journey of transforming leaders, forging excellence, and winning the battle for human flourishing.

··· Bibliography

Aristotle. *Nicomachean Ethics*. Oxford: Oxford University Press, 2009.

Berghaus, Paul, and Nathan Cartegena. "Developing Good Soldiers: The Problem of Fragmentation in the Army." Journal of Military Ethics 12, no. 4 (January 20, 2014): 287–303.

Department of Defense. "2014 Demographics Profile of the Military Community." 2014 Demographics Profile of the Military Community, 2014. *http://download.militaryonesource.mil/12038/MOS/Reports/2014-Demographics-Report.pdf*.

Eagleton, Terry. "Culture and Barbarism: Metaphysics in a Time of Terrorism." Commonweal, March 27, 2009.

French, Shannon. *The Code of the Warrior*. Maryland: Rowman & Littlefield, 2017.

Gilligan, Carol. "In a Different Voice: Women's Conceptions of Self and of Morality." Harvard Educational Review, 1977, 47(4), 481–517.

Goleman, Daniel, Richard Boyatzis, and Annie McKee. Primal Leadership. Boston: Harvard Business School Press, 2002.

Guinness, Os. *The Last Call for Liberty: How America's Genius for Freedom Has Become Its Greatest Threat. Downers Grove*: IVP, 2018.

Hare, John E. *Why Bother Being Good? The Place of God in the Moral Life*. Eugene, OR: InterVarsity Press, 2002.

Hays, Richard B. *The Moral Vision of the New Testament*. New York: Harper Collins, 1996.

"Http://Cape.Army.Mil/Mission.Php," n.d. http://cape.army.mil/mission.php.

Kaurin, Pauline. "Professional Disobedience: Loyalty and the Military by Pauline Shanks Kaurin, Real Clear Defense 08 August 2017." Real Clear Defense, August 8, 2017.

Koontz, Andy. "Infantry OSUT and the First Hundred Yards," May 29, 2020.

Kraft, Dave. *Leaders Who Last*. Wheaton: Crossway, 2010.

Kuhmerker, Lisa, Uwe Gielen, and Richard Hayes. *The Kohlberg Legacy for the Helping Professions*. Birmingham: Doxa, 1991.

Laporta, Jim. "7 Things You Need to Know about the West Point Communist Saga." *www.conservativereview.com*, September 30, 2017.

Ludwig, Dean, and Clinton Longenecker. "The Bathsheba Syndrome: The Ethical Failure of Successful Leaders." Journal of Business Ethics 12 (1993): 265–73.

MacIntyre, Alasdair. *After Virtue*. Notre Dame: University of Notre Dame Press, 1984.

Mattison, William. *Introducing Moral Theology: True Happiness and the Virtues*. Grand Rapids, Michigan: Brazos Press, 2008.

McCullough, David. *John Adams*. New York: Simon & Schuster, 2001.

Morgan, Forrest. *Living the Martial Way: A Manual for the Way a Modern Warrior Should Think*. New Jersey: Barricade Books, 1992.

Nicholson, Lucy. "Military Turns down 80 Percent of Applicants as Armed Forces Shrink." *www.rt.com*, May 15, 2014. *www.rt.com/usa/158992-military-80-percent-rejection-rate*.

Pressfield, Steven. *Gates of Fire*. New York: Bantam, 1998.

Randall, Anthony. "Transformational Moral Leadership and the Army Human Dimension Strategy 2015." Emory University, 2016. "MCOE Transformational Moral Leadership POI." Fort Benning, GA, September 2016. "ET703 Church and Religion in the Public Square," August 21, 2019.

Shay, Jonathan. *Achilles in Vietnam: Combat Trauma and the Undoing of Character*. New York: Simon & Schuster, 1994.

Sigmund, Paul E. ed. *St. Thomas Aquinas on Politics and Ethics*. A Norton Critical Edition. New York: W.W. Norton and Company, 1988.

Volf, Miroslav. *A Public Faith: How Followers of Christ Should Serve the Common Good*. Grand Rapids, Michigan: Brazos Press, 2011.

Warner, Michael, ed. *American Sermons: The Pilgrims to Martin Luther King Jr*. Third. Vol. American Sermons. New York: The Library of America, 1999.

Watkins, Shanea, and James Sherk. "Who Serves in the U.S. Military? The Demographics of Enlisted Troops and Officers," August 21, 2008. http://www.heritage.org/research/reports/2008/08/who-serves-in-the-us-military-the-demographics-of-enlisted-troops-and-officers.

Wells, Samuel. *Improvisation: The Drama of Christian Ethics*. Grand Rapids, Michigan: Brazos Press, 2004.

Westminster Assembly. *The Westminster Confession of Faith: With Proof Texts*. Horsham, PA: Great Commission Publications, 1992.

Wong, Leonard, and Stephen Gerras. "Lying to Ourselves: Dishonesty in the Army Profession." Strategic Studies Institute and US Army War College Press, September 9, 2016.

Wright, N. T. *What St. Paul Really Said*. Grand Rapids: W. B. Eerdmans, 1997.

Zimbardo, Phillip. *The Lucifer Effect: Understanding How Good People Turn Evil*. New York: Random House, 2007

··· Acknowledgments

I would like to express my sincere appreciation and gratitude to the leaders of the United States Army's Maneuver Center of Excellence from 2016-2019 for placing their trust in my professional role as the MCOE Ethics Instructor Chaplain and empowering and enabling the implementation of Transformational Moral Leadership and Ethics.

I am indebted to the visionary leadership of LTG Eric Wesley and LTG Chris Donahue for enabling me to just make it happen; to Dr. Jay Brimstin's ever watchful eye; for COL Timothy Davis, COL Al Leth, COL Robert Fouche, and the Combined Arms Tactics Directorate's friendship and support; The Army Research Institute's Dr. Jennifer Tucker, Dr. Elisabeth Uhl, Dr. Frederick Diedrich, Dr. Tatiana Toumbeva, and Mr. Scott Flanagan for their tireless collaboration, research, and friendship; and CH (COL) David Wake, CH (COL) Michael Jeffries, and CH (LTC) Seth George for their spiritual mantle of leadership over the US Army Chaplaincy's Ethics Community of Practice. To Chaplain (LTC) Jared Vineyard, thank you for your collective passion, like mindedness, and stewardship of the transformational moral leadership process and moving it forward.

To Dennis Jeffrey, Dr. Robert Franklin, and Dr. Reggie McNeal for shaping me as a Transformational Kingdom Leader. To my dearest Brothers and Sisters in Arms, Ranger Chaplains, and BFAM – CH (LTC) USA, RET. Mark Winton, CH (COL) USA, RET. Jim Murphy and Tom Waynick, thank you for always praying, encouraging, and challenging me to choose the hard routine.

To Sensei Emilio Claudio, Dr. Nate Zinnser, and Professor Jason Keaton for teaching and training my warrior ethos, mindset, and martial way. To my Brazilian jui-jitsu family that challenges and humbles the "Fightin Chap," every roll, Respect!

To Neal Huntington, Clint Hurdle, Dave Jauss, Kyle Stark, Larry Broadway, Larry Sutton, Kory DeHaan, Dave Turgeon, Bernie Holliday, Tyson Holt, Todd Tomcyck, Brendan Huttman, David Eckstein, Steve Shenbaum, Rod Olson, John Blanchard, and the entire Pirates Family 2013-2020, thank you for including me as a faithful friend of the program. To our Vanguard XXI team! It is an honor to serve with you and do life together! May we continue to transform leaders, forge excellence, and win!

To my marketplace clients and friends, thank you for entrusting me with your people and organizations and their leadership development, coaching, and growth. To the thousands of leaders who collaborate, participate, and engage in the leadership development and coaching process … continue to practice excellence and permanence as you pursue your passion, purpose, precision.

To those who are fulfilling the call to our profession of arms as Trusted Professionals, to include my children, "to support and defend the Constitution of the United States against all enemies both foreign and domestic, bearing true faith and allegiance to the same" as transformational moral leaders, may God give you courage, wisdom, justice, temperance, faith, hope, and love. Integritas. Strength and Honor.

To E.P. House and Kristin Bentley, thank you for making this possible.

··· About the Author

Dr. Anthony Randall transforms leaders and forges organizational excellence through leadership development and executive coaching as Vanguard XXI's President/Founder. He has taught, trained, and coached over 15,000 professionals across the US Army, Special Operations Units, Major League Baseball, NCAA Division I sports, Fortune 100 and 500 companies, health care, higher education, law enforcement, and the church. He is also an International Coaching Federation (ICF) Professional Certified Coach (PCC), and proprietor of two ICF Credentialed Professional Coaching Courses.

A graduate of the United States Military Academy, West Point, Anthony is an Army Ranger, Chaplain, and retired Lieutenant Colonel. He has six combat tours to Iraq and Afghanistan. He holds two master's degrees in theology and ethics, and a Doctor of Ministry in Leadership. Anthony served fifteen years as a US Army Chaplain for Ranger, Special Forces, and Special Missions; four years as a Law Enforcement Chaplain; and eight years as Chaplain serving the Pittsburgh Pirates.

He holds Japanese Jiu-jitsu and Tae Kwon Do Black Belts, and a Brazilian Jiu-jitsu Purple Belt.

Printed in the USA
CPSIA information can be obtained
at www.ICGtesting.com
CBHW011649051024
15371CB00051B/1626